Bitter Ashes

The Story of WW II

by

John Wilson

Series editor: Allister Thompson

Napoleon Publishing

Napoleon Publishing
an imprint of Napoleon & Company
www.napoleonandcompany.com
Toronto Ontario Canada

Le Conseil des Arts | The Canada Cou
du Canada | for the Arts

Canada

Napoleon & Company acknowledges
the support of the Canada Council for the Arts
for our publishing program. We acknowledge the support of the
Government of Canada through the Book Publishing Industry
Development Program (BPIDP) for our publishing activities.

Manufactured by Friesens Corporation in Altona, Canada
December 2009

13 12 11 10 09   5 4 3 2 1

Library and Archives Canada Cataloguing in Publication

Wilson, John (John Alexander), 1951-
        Bitter ashes : the story of WW II / John Wilson.

(Stories of Canada)
Includes bibliographical references and index.
ISBN 978-1-894917-90-2

        1. World War, 1939-1945--Juvenile literature.   2. World War, 1939-1945--
Canada--Juvenile literature.   3. Canada--History--1939-1945--Juvenile literature.
4. World War, 1939-1945--Canada--Pictorial works--Juvenile Literature.
I. Title. II. Series: Stories of Canada (Toronto, Ont.)

D743.7.W54 2009   j940.53'71
C2009-904778-0

For the children who died in the war

"Children are not the people of tomorrow, but people today. They are entitled to be taken seriously. They have a right to be treated by adults with tenderness and respect, as equals. They should be allowed to grow into whoever they were meant to be—the unknown person inside each of them is the hope for the future."
                    -Janusz Korczak

(Korczak was in charge of an orphanage in the Warsaw ghetto. Refusing a chance to hide, he chose to accompany his children to the Treblinka death camp.)

Europe after the Treaty of Versailles in 1919

Guernica

The bombers—angular triple-engined Junker 52s and sleek gull-winged Heinkel 111s—swept over the hills from the north. For two-and-a-half hours on the afternoon of April 26, 1937, two dozen planes dropped forty tons of bombs on the undefended town of Guernica in Northern Spain.

The Spanish Civil War was a national conflict with roots far back in Spanish history, but it was also a testing ground for new military technologies, tactics and political ideologies.

Thousands of individuals saw Spain as the beginning of something bigger and volunteered to help as soldiers, nurses and doctors. Among them were almost 1,600 Canadians who defied their own government to take a stand for what they believed in. Half of them never came home and, even today, none of them is commemorated on official war memorials in Canada or recognized in Remembrance Day services.

Panicked refugees fled through the chaos of collapsing buildings. Shards of hot, jagged metal and fragments of walls and furniture flew everywhere. The air was filled with screams and the crackle of fires taking hold amidst the rubble.

The planners, pilots and bomb-aimers that day were mostly German, although they were fighting in the Spanish Civil War. They were there to help the Spanish army, which had revolted against the legal government in July, 1936, and they were there to practice for a much bigger war.

The attack shocked the world and inspired Pablo Picasso to paint one of art's great masterpieces, but it was a small scale tragedy compared with what would happen later to Barcelona, London, Berlin, Dresden, Tokyo and Hiroshima.

Guernica was a beginning. It was also a clear signal that wars were no longer just fought between armies on battlefields. In the coming war, civilian men, women and children would be front-line soldiers.

Pablo Picasso's *Guernica* is reproduced as a wall mural in the modern town.

The Lost Peace

"Freedom is always and exclusively freedom for the one who thinks differently."
-Rosa Luxemburg

Adolf Hitler was famous for his impassioned, angry speeches. He wears the Nazi swastika symbol on his arm.

On the night of January 15, 1919, Rosa Luxemburg, a leader of the new German Communist Party, was led from a police station in Berlin, beaten, shot and her body dumped in the Landwehr Canal.

At the end of WW I, Germany's army was defeated, its navy in revolt and its people starving. Civil war, like the one that was raging in Russia, seemed a certainty. But the German revolution failed. What was left of the army crushed it by killing the leaders such as Rosa Luxemburg, and a democratic government was established.

Unfortunately, much of the bitterness of 1919 simmered beneath the surface and occasionally erupted in violence. Through it all, the average person struggled to survive as German money became worthless and communist workers and police battled each other in the streets.

On July 29, 1921, an ex-corporal with a gift for speech-making became the leader of a small party composed largely of men who had fought against Luxemburg and the German Revolution. They called themselves the National Socialist German Workers' Party and

Italy had not been on the losing side in WW I, but it had suffered and, having only been a unified country since 1870, was as divided by internal tensions as Germany.

Like Hitler, Benito Mussolini was a veteran of WW I. After the war, Mussolini formed the National Fascist Party, which promised stability and a return to the glories of ancient Rome. In 1922 he led his party on a march on Rome and seized power. Shortly afterward, he declared himself supreme ruler, or Il Duce.

Mussolini succeeded because his party, like the Nazis, was violent and well-organized, whereas those opposed to him spent as much time fighting each other as the Fascists.

Hitler admired Mussolini and attempted his own coup in Munich in 1923. It failed, and Hitler spent a year in jail, but his time would come, and by the mid 1930s, both Italy and Germany were solidly fascist and dominated the centre of Europe.

promised to bring law and order to Germany and make it a powerful country once more.

The National Socialist, or Nazi Party, was organized along military lines; its members wore brown uniforms and fought with, threatened and intimidated anyone who disagreed with them. By 1932 they were powerful enough to become the largest party in the German parliament. On January 30, 1933, their leader, Adolf Hitler, became German Chancellor. The following year, he declared himself Führer, or Leader, of Germany. On that day, the freedom to think differently in Germany disappeared, and Nazi ideology, under the direction of Hitler and his propaganda expert, Joseph Goebbels, became the law.

Benito Mussolini

Fascism

Fascism succeeded in countries other than Germany and Italy. For example, the Spanish Civil War established a version of Fascism that lasted until 1975.

In Britain, Oswald Mosley led the British Union of Fascists which, at its height, claimed 50,000 members. In Canada, the Fascists were led by Adrien Arcand and his National Unity Party of Canada, or Blue Shirts. Arcand greatly admired Hitler, and throughout the 1930s his Blue Shirts battled political opponents in the streets of Montreal. Arcand was also anti-semitic, and his party often attacked Jewish businesses and individuals.

While Arcand's Fascists only ever had a few thousand members, they had support in high places. R. B. Bennett, Canadian Prime Minister from 1930 to 1935, was sympathetic and secretly supplied funds.

A propaganda flyer for
Arcand's Blue Shirts

Tens of millions of people died in the 20th century because of three competing political ideas, Capitalism, Communism and Fascism.

Capitalism was prevalent in Europe and North America and encouraged private ownership of goods, trade and a society where different classes had different roles to play based largely on wealth. It usually resulted in a democratic form of government.

Communism encouraged the common ownership of property and factories and a classless society where all were equal. The Communist society set up by the 1917 revolution in Russia developed into a dictatorship where a few people held all the power and allowed no one else to disagree.

Fascism in Italy and Germany grew up as an alternative to the other two systems. Like Communism, it was a dictatorship where the government controlled the economy, but it also allowed large private businesses to flourish as long as they supported the leaders. Fascism was also always strongly nationalistic and told people that it was recreating some glorious period from their county's past; for example, Mussolini said he was recreating the ancient Roman Empire.

Fascism was destroyed in WW II, and Communism, outside China, collapsed in the 1990s. We live, today, in a capitalist world.

Beginning

Why did no one try to stop Hitler earlier? The answer lies in a policy called "appeasement". Many senior politicians in the 1930s had been young soldiers in WW I and were terrified of a repetition of the horrors they had seen and lived through in the trenches. Surely, they reasoned, Hitler could not want that either, so if they gave him what he asked for, he would be reasonable.

This kind of thinking led to Czechoslovakia being handed over to Germany in 1938 and the world watching as German planes experimented over Guernica.

Appeasement was strengthened by several people's false personal impressions of Hitler. When William Lyon McKenzie King, the Canadian Prime minister, returned from visiting Germany in 1937, he confided in his diary that he thought Hitler a "man of deep sincerity," "who truly loves his fellow-men, and his country," and compared the dictator to Joan of Arc. He could hardly have been more wrong.

Chamberlain

Hitler's plans for a Greater Germany required that the country expand. In March 1936, Hitler sent soldiers into the Rhineland, an area of Germany occupied by the Allies after WW I. Although only a few German soldiers crossed the border on bicycles, no one stopped them.

Two years later, Hitler sent his troops into Austria to re-unite the two German-speaking populations. Again no one stopped them.

In September 1938, Hitler demanded that Germany be allowed to control the border areas of Czechoslovakia where large numbers of Germans lived. Neville Chamberlain, Britain's Prime Minister, and the governments of France and Italy, gave in to Hitler, and once more, German soldiers marched. Seven months later, they continued into the rest of Czechoslovakia.

But Czechoslovakia would be the last time the German army would be unopposed. Everyone now knew that Hitler would not stop.

On September 1, 1939, German soldiers and tanks crossed into Poland. Britain asked Germany immediately to withdraw its army. On September 3, Neville Chamberlain went on the radio to announce that since "no such undertaking has been received...consequently, this country is now at war with Germany."

Poland and the Phoney War

The Royal Castle in Warsaw aflame during the Blitzkrieg

A German Panzer

The Polish air force was destroyed on the first day of the German attack, and the Polish capital, Warsaw, fell on September 27, 1939. The speed of the German Blitzkrieg, or Lightning War, shocked everyone and gave Britain and France no time to send help. Instead they concentrated their forces along the French border, waiting for the German attack.

After Poland collapsed, it was, by prior arrangement, split between Germany and Russia (officially called the Union of Soviet Socialist Republics or U.S.S.R.). The German army hurried to the French border to meet the expected attack from there. Nothing happened.

All through the winter of 1939/40, the German, French and British armies sat and looked at each other. There was little fighting between the main armies, but minor campaigns occurred elsewhere.

At the end of November, Russia took the opportunity of the rest of Europe being at war to invade Finland. Despite a disadvantage of two hundred to one, the Finns proved surprisingly dogged defenders, and the war was costly, dragging on until March.

In April, Hitler ordered his armies to invade Denmark and Norway so that Germany could secure iron ore supplies from neutral Sweden. Faced with overwhelming forces, both countries surrendered quickly.

War at Sea

The *Graf Spee* operated in the south Atlantic, sinking nine merchant ships before being brought to battle off Montevideo in Uruguay. After the ship was damaged, the captain ordered the *Graf Spee* sunk on December 17, 1939.

The *Bismarck*

While the armies faced each other on land, battles were raging at sea. Although German plans to starve Britain mainly involved submarines, or U-boats, Germany had several surface raiders whose job was to attack merchant ships. The most famous of these were the *Admiral Graf Spee* and the *Bismarck*.

A serious threat occurred in May 1940, when the *Bismarck*, at the time the largest commissioned warship in the world, broke out into the Atlantic. Exhibiting the power of its eight 15- inch guns, the *Bismarck* sank the British battle cruiser HMS *Hood* in a matter of minutes.

British Prime Minister Winston Churchill ordered that the *Bismarck* be hunted down, and a chase around the north Atlantic began. Eventually, the *Bismarck*'s steering was damaged and its speed reduced in almost suicidal torpedo attacks by antiquated biplanes. This allowed the British fleet to catch and severely damage it. Badly damaged, the *Bismarck*'s crew sank it late in the morning of May 27.

With the sinking of the *Bismarck*, the serious threat from surface raiders was over. The much more deadly underwater threat was just about to begin.

Unlike 1914, in 1939 Canada was not bound to go to war when Britain did. However, the prime minister, McKenzie King, called on parliament to debate the issue, and war was declared on September 10.

Part of the First Canadian Infantry Division, stationed in Britain, was landed in France after the evacuation of Dunkirk, but they were pulled out almost immediately. After that, they spent the summer marching all across southern England to fool German intelligence into thinking there were more troops than there really were.

Almost three hundred Canadians served in the British airforce in the early days of WW II, both as fighter pilots and bomber crews. Sixteen of them flew in the all-Canadian 242 Squadron in France and later in the Battle of Britain.

The most successful was a man from Calgary named Willie McKnight. Flying Hurricanes in France and Spitfires over England, McKnight officially shot down seventeen enemy aircraft, on several occasions three in a single day, before he went missing on a flight over occupied France on January 12, 1941. He was twenty-three years old.

The Real Thing

All through the winter, while the armies stared at each other, weapons were being frantically manufactured, soldiers trained and plans made. On the night of May 10, 1940, German forces attacked the Netherlands, Belgium and France.

The Germans attacked with 3,000,000 men, 2,700 tanks and self-propelled guns, 7,500 artillery pieces and 5,000 combat aircraft. To oppose them, the French and British could call on 6,000,000 men, 6,000 tanks and self-propelled guns, 14,000 artillery pieces and 2,600 combat aircraft. The Allies were stronger, but the Germans had two huge advantages—they had more and better planes and dominated the skies over France from the first days of the attack. They concentrated their tanks into Panzer Divisions rather than spread them about amongst the infantry.

Led by two brilliant and impetuous tank commanders, Erwin Rommel and Heinz Guderian, hundreds of Panzer Mark III and IV tanks sped across the French countryside toward the English Channel, trapping the

Rommel

8

Scenes from the
evacuation of Dunkirk

French and British Armies in the north. Rommel and Guderian succeeded by driving their tanks hard and not waiting for artillery and infantry support. They relied on the German airforce, the Luftwaffe, and their terrifying Stuka dive bombers to clear their way and break up any counter-attacks.

It was dangerous, but the speed of the advance shocked and confused the French commanders. As defences collapsed in late May, the remains of the British army in France were evacuated from Dunkirk. On June 14, Paris fell, and eight days later the French signed an armistice in the same railway carriage where the Germans had signed the treaty to end WW I in 1918. As the new British Prime Minister, Winston Churchill, pointed out, the Battle of France was over and the Battle of Britain about to begin.

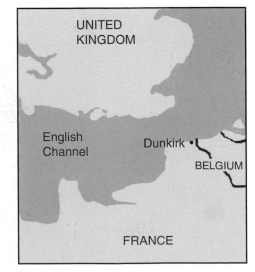

The Few

With his instantly recognizable physique and cigar, Winston Churchill came to symbolize British resistance to Hitler in 1940. His speeches, like the one on the Few, were often inspirational masterpieces.

When Britain stood alone after France fell, he said: "We shall go on to the end...we shall defend our island, whatever the cost may be. We shall fight on the beaches, we shall fight on the landing grounds, we shall fight in the fields and in the streets, we shall fight in the hills; we shall never surrender."

Shortly after, he said: "Hitler knows that he will have to break us in this island or lose the war. If we can stand up to him, all Europe may be free...if we fail then the whole world...will sink into the abyss of a new dark age... Let us therefore brace ourselves to our duty, and so bear ourselves that, if the British Commonwealth and its Empire lasts for a thousand years, men will still say, 'This was their finest hour'."

After France collapsed, Hitler hoped that Britain would make peace. However, as the German tanks rolled into Belgium on May 10, a new Prime Minister had taken over promising that he had nothing to give but "blood, toil, tears and sweat." Winston Churchill had been opposed to the policy of appeasement for some time.

Hitler ordered an invasion of southern England, Operation Sealion, but there was something that had to happen first. If the invasion fleet was not to be sunk in the English Channel, the Luftwaffe had to control the skies. They began on July 10 by attacking ships off the British coast.

The convoy battles lasted a month and provided both sides with experience, but the crucial phase lasted from August 12 to September 6. For almost four weeks of glorious summer weather, a vital battle raged in the skies over

To the Canadian Parliament in December 1941, Churchill recalled May 1940: "When I warned them (the French Government) that Britain would fight on alone whatever they did, their generals told their Prime Minister...'In three weeks England will have her neck wrung like a chicken.' Some chicken! Some neck!"

10

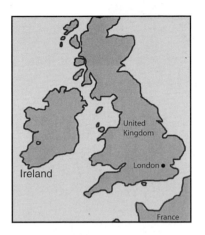

A British Spitfire fighter plane

southern England. The Germans bombed fighter airfields, production factories and the indispensable radar stations that gave the RAF pilots warning of coming attacks.

Despite huge losses of aircraft and, more importantly, experienced pilots, the RAF held on. Day after day, British, Canadian, Australian, South African, Polish, Czechoslovak and French pilots took their Hurricanes and Spitfires into the summer skies to shoot down the German Heinkels and Messerschmitts.

As time went on, it became obvious that the Luftwaffe was not gaining superiority. On August 25, German bombers strayed over London. Churchill ordered an attack on Berlin the following night. The Berlin raid was small, but an enraged Hitler ordered more attacks on British cities. The hard-pressed RAF got a breather, and in subsequent weeks began to get the upper hand against the German attacks. The Battle of Britain was won. On September 17, Hitler postponed Operation Sealion indefinitely.

Of the fighter and bomber crews who handed Germany its first defeat of the war, Churchill said: "Never in the field of human conflict was so much owed by so many to so few."

London children amongst the rubble

Blitz

One British response to the threat of invasion and bombing was evacuation. Between the outbreak of war and the Battle of Britain, some 1.5 million people, over half of them children, were sent to live in the countryside, where they were billeted in private homes. In addition to this official evacuation, another 2 million were evacuated privately.

In May 1940, a scheme to evacuate children out of Britain, many to Canada was begun. A shortage of ships slowed this evacuation, and the plan was abandoned in September when the ship the *City of Benares* was torpedoed, and *77* of the 90 child evacuees were killed.

People taking shelter in the London subway system

On September 7, 364 German bombers, more than ten times the number that attacked Guernica, bombed the east end of London in an attempt to force Britain to make peace. The bombs killed 436 people, but it was only the beginning. For 57 nights in a row, the bombers returned.

Every night, the sirens wailed and people fled to backyard air raid shelters or subway stations. Except for the flames, London became a city of darkness. Wardens patrolled the deserted streets looking for any light that might give the bombers above a target. Volunteers struggled to dig survivors and bodies out of the rubble.

Searchlights criss-crossed the sky, and anti-aircraft guns, set up on any piece of open ground, pounded away. They did little good other than giving the suffering populace the sense that they were fighting back.

From November on, the bombers began targeting other cities as well as London: Coventry, Liverpool, Manchester, Bristol, Glasgow. By May 1941, more than 43,000 civilians were dead, and cities all over Britain were in ruins. But Britain hadn't surrendered and, although no one knew it at the time, the battle in the night skies was over. Even as Londoners were huddling in their shelters, Hitler and his generals were planning a move that would expand the war immeasurably.

Battle of the Atlantic

The Royal Canadian Navy (RCN) began WW II with only six destroyers. By 1945, the RCN was the third largest fleet in the world. In between, it sank 28 submarines and numerous surface vessels, and played a major role in protecting the vital convoys of ships carrying supplies to Britain.

A WW II German U-Boat on display as a tourist attraction in Kiel, Germany

As an island surrounded by enemies, Britain needed more than a million tons of imported food and material every week. If that supply was cut off, the war was lost.

In the early years of the war, the German U-boats, and Italian ones after Mussolini's declaration of war in June 1940, had a huge advantage. Fortunately, a focus in Germany before the war on building battleships meant that there were not many U-boats available.

As the number of U-boats increased, the tactics to combat them improved. Convoys assembled in Halifax were protected by the rapidly growing Canadian navy, equipped with better ships and more efficient ways of detecting and sinking the enemy.

The Battle of the Atlantic lasted for the entire war, with first one side then the other having the advantage. It was also a brutal struggle, as 3,500 Allied ships and 780 U-boats were sunk. Two thousand Canadian sailors and 1,600 merchant seamen never came home.

13

Canada's Contribution

Canada's contribution to the struggle in the north Atlantic was not simply sailors, ships and escorts. It was also what was put in the holds of the ships, and that was not just food to keep beleaguered Britain going.

In 1938, the Canadian automotive industry was the fourth largest in the world. Once it geared up for war, the flow of trucks for the war effort was almost endless. During WW II, Canada produced 800,000 trucks, half those used by the British Army, an amount second only to the United States and exceeding the total combined output of Germany, Italy and Japan.

Canada also produced 16,000 fighters and bomber aircraft, 345 merchant ships, destroyers, corvette, frigates and, perhaps most importantly in a modern mechanized war, half the aluminum and ninety per cent of the nickel used by the Allies.

Even in the first difficult years of the war, Canadian industry was sowing the industrial seeds that, four years down the road, would enable eventual victory for the Allies.

Looking East

On May 10, 1941, as Hitler was finalizing his plans for the invasion of Russia, a lone figure parachuted from a German plane over the west of Scotland. To the surprised farmer who arrested him, the man claimed to be Hitler's second-in-command, Rudolf Hess. He said he had arrived to negotiate peace and that Germany would give back all its conquered territory in western Europe if Britain would help in the coming war against Russia.

Because he was kept alone in prison long after all the other Nazis were released and because the files relating to his flight are still secret, theories abound about the real reason for his flight.

The main ones are that there was a group in Britain who wanted to make peace and were prepared to take over the government from Churchill or, more likely, that Hess was tricked into coming by the British Secret Service. In any case, nothing came of the flight, and Hess was tried for war crimes in 1946. He committed suicide in prison in 1987 at the age of ninety-three.

Hess

Only days before Hitler invaded Poland, he and the Russian leader, Joseph Stalin, had signed a treaty. In it, they agreed publicly not to attack each other and privately to split Poland between them. It was a cynical agreement, and neither expected it to last.

As early as 1924, Hitler had stated that Germany's future lay in conquering the lands to the east, enslaving the people there and exploiting the farmland and oil reserves. In December 1940, planning began for a massive attack designed to defeat Russia in a single summer. The attack was codenamed Operation Barbarossa.

Unable to decide between a northern attack toward Leningrad, a central thrust at Moscow or a southern advance into the Ukraine, German planners opted for all three. They believed that such a huge attack was possible because they had succeed so easily in France, Russia had struggled against tiny Finland, and Stalin had removed many of his top generals in purges in the late 1930s.

The attack was planned for the spring of 1941. Meanwhile, Hitler sent his armies to help Mussolini by invading Yugoslavia and Greece. As soon as that was accomplished and the spring thaw in Eastern Europe was over, three million soldiers, four Panzer groups and three air fleets, divided into three Army Groups, launched the largest military operation in human history.

Barbarossa

"The struggle will have to be conducted with unprecedented, unmerciful and unrelenting harshness…commissars will be liquidated. German soldiers guilty of breaking international law…will be excused."

Adolf Hitler
March 30, 1941

At nine p.m. on Saturday, June 21, 1941, Alfred Liskow, a German soldier from Munich, slipped across the border and told his Russian captors that the German invasion of Russia was due to start at four a.m. the next day. Word was passed to Stalin in Moscow, who ordered Liskow shot for lying. At 3:15 a.m. on Sunday, the German guns opened up.

As the Panzers raced forward in the dawn light, the Russian defences collapsed. Communications failed, and most of the front line defences and the air force were destroyed. In the first weeks, huge pincer movements encircled and captured hundreds of thousands of Russians. It all seemed easy.

As Hitler's armies raced forward, led by Guderian's tanks, communications and supply lines became stretched, soldiers became exhausted and machines broke down. On top of it all, the Russians were proving tougher opponents than expected.

All three fronts could not be maintained at the same time. Decisions would have to be made.

The war in the east was not the same as the war in the west. It was a war of ideology, Fascism against Communism, and twisted racism, Aryan against Slav.

Hitler and many of the other Nazi leaders believed that they were fighting to produce a master race that would dominate Europe. It was a dangerous fantasy that encouraged Germans to see themselves as superior to all other "lesser" races. In particular, the Slavic peoples of Russia were considered subhuman and were to be enslaved and exterminated in order to create living space for "pure" Aryans.

Captured soldiers were often shot out of hand or sent back as slave labourers to be worked to death. Civilians were routinely massacred. In all, between 1941 and 1945, the war in the east killed thirty million people.

Guderian wanted to concentrate on Moscow, the capital. Hitler decided to stop the attack on Moscow in order to strengthen the other two attacks. In the north, Leningrad was reached in August, but the defences were too strong, and Hitler decided to try to starve the city. In the south, Kiev was taken, but Russia seemed endless.

On October 2, the focus was switched back to Moscow. The Panzers again raced forward, but rain turned the roads to mud and sometimes slowed the advance to a kilometre or two a day. This was fatal for Blitzkreig and allowed defences to be prepared and fresh Russian troops to be brought in from Siberia.

In November, the ground froze, and the tanks moved so close to Moscow that German officers could see the downtown through their field glasses. Then the temperature dropped to -20 or -30 degrees Celsius. The Germans, without winter clothing, froze. The attack stalled. On December 5, Guderian wrote, "The offensive on Moscow has ended." It was time for the Russians to hit back.

This chilling photo titled "The Last Jew in Vinnitsa" shows the atrocities the Nazis were capable of.

Counterattack

Another problem the Germans had in the winter of 1941/42 was dealing with partisans, guerrilla fighters hiding and waiting to strike at their forces.

The huge battles of encirclement during the summer meant that large numbers of Russian soldiers had escaped into the vast forests of the western U.S.S.R. Gradually they became organized and began to hit back at German supplies and communications.

A supply convoy could never know when shells and bullets would erupt from the surrounding woods, destroying vehicles and killing men. Torn up railway lines and downed telephone lines caused all sorts of problems for the soldiers facing the T-34s outside Moscow. The Germans used precious resources combing the forests and attempted to terrify the locals by mass shootings of hostages but, in four years of war, they never solved the partisan problem.

As the Germans stood at the gates of Moscow, nursing frostbitten hands and feet, the Siberian army rushed from the far side of Russia and dressed for the weather, attacked.

The Germans fought bitterly, but the fresh Russian troops were well supplied. They had warm, camouflaged winter clothing and they had T-34 tanks and Katyusha rocket launchers.

The T-34 was a shock to the German tank commanders in 1941. It was more powerful and had a longer range than the German tanks, and its better suspension and wider tracks meant that it worked far better in mud and snow. The Russians also had a KV1 tank that the Germans were horrified to see their shells bounce off, but there were too few to make a difference.

The Katyusha was a bank of rockets mounted on a truck. Several of them firing at the same time could deliver a stunning amount of high explosives onto an enemy position. Because of the whine the rockets made when launched, the Germans called them "Stalin's organ pipes".

A T-34 tank

Over the winter, the fresh troops and new weapons pushed the invaders back from Moscow. Operation Barbarossa had failed, and Moscow was safe; Leningrad was besieged but hadn't fallen. The German army still held vast areas of Russia, but it had suffered its first major defeat. When the spring came in 1942, could they recover the initiative? Should they try to attack Moscow again, or should they head farther south toward the rich oilfields of the Caucasus?

Russian forces were much better prepared for winter conditions.

In China, a well-organized Communist Party, led by Mao Zedong, fought effectively against the Japanese invaders. They were helped by an extraordinary Canadian, Doctor Norman Bethune.

Bethune had been a stretcher-bearer in WW I and an innovator in the treatment of tuberculosis in Montreal in the early 1930s. His socialist views made him an early proponent of universal medicare, and, in 1937, took him to Spain to help the government fight against the Fascists. In 1938, he went to China.

Bethune set up medical services to care for the Chinese soldiers fighting for Mao. Often under Japanese fire, he worked tirelessly at his mobile operating table to save lives.

In late 1939, Bethune cut his finger while operating and developed blood poisoning. He died on November 12.

Bethune is regarded as a hero in China and has many statues and a memorial hall dedicated to him. In Canada, the house where he was born in Gravenhurst, Ontario is a museum and National Historic Site.

Bethune in China

Another War

The reason Stalin could bring his Siberian army to relieve Moscow was that one of his spies in Tokyo had discovered that Japan was not planning to attack Russia, but was looking elsewhere.

Japanese industry had expanded dramatically in the 20th century. To sustain it, Japan needed raw materials, mainly oil, that were not available in its home islands. The men in power in Tokyo felt that the way to secure these supplies was by military conquest.

By 1941, Japan had a powerful army, navy and air force, all supplied with some of the most efficient guns, ships and planes in the world. It had shocked everyone by defeating Russia in 1905, fought on the Allied side in WW I and had been fighting a successful four-year-long war in China.

Japan had also signed a pact with Germany. Tokyo's military leaders, led by General Hideki Tojo, felt that the time was ripe to take on their main Pacific rival, the United States.

Tojo

Pearl Harbor

Fleet Admiral Isoroku Yamamoto was in an impossible position. He knew that Japan couldn't win an extended war against the industrial might of the United States, yet he was forced to plan one by his government. Japan's only chance, Yamamoto said, was to destroy American naval power in the Pacific suddenly and force a peace.

The attack on Pearl Harbor almost succeeded but, from Japan's point of view, two things went wrong.

First, the American aircraft carriers were not in dock and so were not sunk. Second, a proposed third wave attack against Hawaii's dry docks, ship repair facilities and fuel depots was cancelled.

Had the aircraft carriers been sunk and the docks and fuel supplies destroyed, it would have been much more difficult for the U.S. to respond to Japan's aggression in the Pacific. Japan would not have won the war, but it would have been longer and harder. As Japanese Admiral Hara Tadaichi said, "We won a great tactical victory at Pearl Harbor and thereby lost the war."

Early on the morning of Sunday, December 7th, 1941, Privates Joseph Lockard and George Elliot were practicing with the new radar installations at Opana Point on the island of Oahu in Hawaii. At 7:02, they spotted a large mass of aircraft heading for the islands. The puzzled men reported their findings to Lieutenant Kermit Tyler, who assumed the activity was a returning flight of American bombers and told the men not to worry. Thus the chance was lost to give almost an hour's warning of one of the greatest surprise attacks in history.

The image that Lockard and Elliot saw was actually the first wave of 183 Japanese bombers, torpedo bombers and fighters sweeping in on Oahu from six undetected aircraft carriers to the north. Their intention was to destroy the American fleet at anchor in the naval base at Pearl Harbor. Shortly before eight o'clock, the first bombers roared in toward the American battleships parked in a neat row in the middle of the harbor. At the same time, other bombers and fighters destroyed American planes parked in the open on airfields across the island.

A second wave followed the first, and ninety minutes after it began, the attack was over. Five battleships and thirteen other ships were sunk, and three hundred planes either destroyed or damaged. American dead numbered 2,386, more than half killed when the battleship USS *Arizona* blew up.

America was suddenly at war, and December 7, 1941 had become, as President Roosevelt said, "A date which will live in infamy."

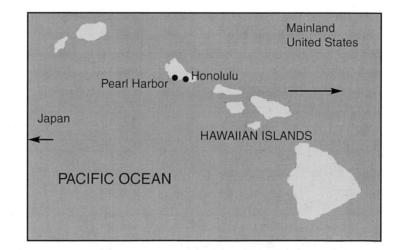

Scenes from the attack on Pearl Harbor

Internment

Racism was a factor in the war in the Pacific. It was fuelled by fear, hatred and a sense that the other side was "them" and very different from "us".

Certainly there were huge cultural differences between North Americans and Japanese people. For example, a Japanese sailor from a submarine that was part of the attack on Pearl Harbor was captured alive. To be captured was a great dishonour, and the sailor decided to commit suicide. However, he felt he couldn't carry it out without the permission of his jailers. Throughout the war, the sailor repeatedly asked his guards if he could commit suicide, and they refused. The sailor survived the war.

The attack on Pearl Harbor created panic all along the west coast. Suddenly, the 22,000 Japanese Canadians in British Columbia, many of whom had lived there all their lives, and some of whom were decorated veterans of WW I, were potential enemies. Although the army and police didn't see them as a threat, the government gave in to public pressure and declared a zone, 160 kilometres inland from the coast, which was to be made free from those of Japanese descent.

All Japanese Canadians, whether full citizens or not, were moved to internment camps in the B.C. interior or to work projects on the prairies. Even after Japan was defeated, the government tried to move all Japanese Canadians out of B.C. for good. Public protests eventually stopped it, but not before four thousand people were deported to Japan.

The Japanese in B.C. were no threat, but the resettlement was a response to strong anti-Japanese racism in B.C. Most Japanese property, fishing boats, farms, houses, and any furniture too big to take to the camps, was seized and sold at rock-bottom prices. A lot of people made a lot of money out of the Japanese internment.

In 1988, Prime Minister Brian Mulroney formally apologized for the government's actions and announced a large compensation package for surviving internees and their families.

Japanese Canadians on their way to deportation

23

Hong Kong

The first Victoria Cross of the war, a medal for bravery, was awarded after the battle for Hong Kong.

Company Sergeant-Major John Robert Osborn of the Winnipeg Grenadiers spent the morning of December 19 leading his company in fighting off Japanese attacks. Eventually, they were forced to withdraw.

That afternoon, Osborn's company was again attacked, and several grenades were thrown into their position. Osborn hurled most back, but one lodged in a place where he could not retrieve it. Shouting a warning to his companions, Sergeant Osborn threw himself on top of the grenade.

It exploded, killing Osborn instantly, but his body absorbed the explosion and saved the lives of those around him.

Apart from fighter and bomber crews in Europe and protecting convoys in the Atlantic, Canadian soldiers had not been involved yet in the war. That changed when the Japanese invaded Hong Kong. Two Canadian units, the Royal Rifles of Canada and the Winnipeg Grenadiers, took part in the seventeen-day defence of the colony. They were outnumbered and ultimately overrun on Christmas Day, 1941. Those not killed in the fighting could only look forward to many years of brutal imprisonment.

Personnel of the Royal Rifles of Canada
and mascot en route to Hong Kong

24

World War

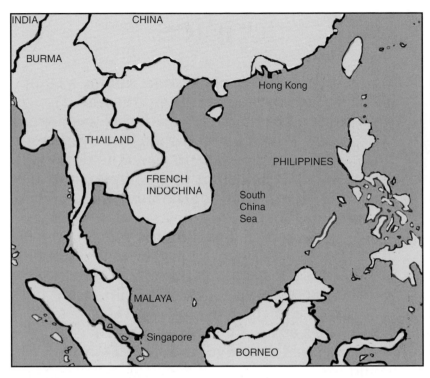

In the days after Pearl Harbor, Japanese forces attacked Thailand, Malaya, the Philippines, Hong Kong, Burma, Guam, Wake Island, Borneo and Singapore. On the morning of December 10th, the British battleship *Prince of Wales* and the battlecruiser *Repulse* were sunk by Japanese planes off the coast of Malaya. On December 11, Germany and Italy declared war on the United States.

The war was now a true world war, and the entry of America on the Allied side probably ensured eventual victory, but as 1941 ended, the Axis Powers held the upper hand. Germany had conquered Western Europe, dominated the Mediterranean and stood at the gates of Moscow and Leningrad. The Japanese Empire was spreading, apparently unstoppably, across the Pacific and toward India and Australia. But there were glimmers of hope for the Allies. Russia had not collapsed under the first brutal onslaught of Operation Barbarossa, and the industrial power of America was now on their side.

Substitution codes have been used at least since Julius Caesar fought in Gaul more than two thousand years ago. They are based on substituting one letter of the alphabet for another. For example:

```
ABCDEFGHIJKLMNOPQRSTUVWXYZABCDEFGHI
  ABCDEFGHIJKLMNOPQRSTUVWXYZ
```

In the above example, E becomes A, F becomes B, etc. Thus ATTACK becomes WPPWYG. The problem is, all you need to break the code is to know what letter A corresponds to in the substitution alphabet, and there are only 26 possibilities. Try to break this code: NAPNAWP

You can make it more complex by mixing up the letters of the alphabet, but code-breakers would still find it very easy to read. What Enigma did was to use a number of electrically triggered wheels to create several levels of substitution, making it almost unbreakable without an example of the machine and code books—like the one captured from *U-110*.

Spies

Spying, from sneaking into the enemy's camp to overhear his plans, to the pilot who spotted the German army swinging away from Paris in 1914, has always been important in war. It is doubly important in a complex global conflict where technological advances are being made almost daily.

In WW II, radio made communication over great distances much easier and more secure than it had been in any previous war. There were no wires to be cut by partisans or shellfire, and it was possible to communicate with ships and submarines at sea almost instantly. The downside was that anyone else with a receiver could listen in, hence the need for complex codes so that no one but the receiver could understand what was being sent.

In the 1920s and 30s, the Germans developed a series of immensely complex code machines that made breaking codes almost impossible. Called Enigma, these machines used a substitution cipher (explained in the sidebar). The German air force, army and navy used different versions of Enigma and believed it to be virtually unbreakable. It was not.

The Enigma machine

With help from Polish code-breakers, the Allies could read the German airforce and army codes early in the war, but the naval code proved more troublesome.

On May 9, 1941, U-boat *U-110* attacked convoy C.B.318 south of Iceland. The U-boat was seriously damaged and forced to the surface, where it was attacked by a destroyer, HMS *Bulldog.* Thinking his boat was sinking, The captain, Fritz-Julius Lemp, ordered the crew to abandon ship, leaving secret code books and an Enigma code machine on board.

When the captain realized that the *U-110* wasn't sinking, he tried to swim back but was shot by a British sailor.

The captured Enigma machine and code books were sent to Britain, where they helped decipher the German naval code, enabling the Allies to read all messages from the German Navy to their U-boats.

The captain's failure to destroy his Enigma machine was a major turning point in the intelligence war. The capture of *U-110* was used as the basis for the 2000 movie *U-571.*

The SS (short for Schutzstaffel, which means "Protective Squadron") began as Hitler's personal bodyguard. Fanatically loyal to Hitler personally, it grew into a force of over a million men whose responsibilities included security, espionage, fighting on the front line and the carrying out of the horrific plans outlined at Wannsee.

Heydrich did not long survive the Wannsee meeting. In Prague on May 27, 1942, two British-trained Czech assassins attacked his car. Eight days later, Heydrich died of his wounds.

On June 9, as a reprisal for Heydrich's death, the Germans obliterated the village of Lidice in Czechoslovakia, killing every man and sending the women and children to concentration camps. Even in death, Heydrich was still a killer.

Himmler

Wannsee Conference

As the Panzers raced across Russia in 1941, Hitler's mind turned to the millions of European Jews who were now under German control. Hitler, and many of the other top Nazis, were violently anti-semitic. They saw Jews as subhuman and the cause of all of Germany's problems. Now that the Nazis had conquered a huge area of Europe, they planned to put their twisted ideas of racial superiority into practice.

Hitler and Heinrich Himmler, the head of the SS, knew what they wanted to do—to kill every single Jew in Europe. It is hard to imagine how anyone could create the horror of attempting to murder millions of innocent men, women and children, but Hitler and Himmler did, and they had the power to do it.

Already by 1941, mobile murder squads, called "Einsatzgruppen", were following the army into Russia and shooting and gassing tens of thousands of Jews, but to kill millions of people required much more planning and organization. Reinhard Heydrich, Himmler's deputy in the SS, was given the task of planning the horror.

On January 20th, 1942, fifteen officials led by Heydrich met at a villa in the Berlin suburb of Wannsee. Present were representatives

The Fascist leaders, including Mussolini, Hess, Hitler and Himmler, in 1938

The Nazis forced Jews to identify themselves with this badge.

from Ministries of the Interior and Justice, Security and the governments of the occupied territories. Minutes of the meeting were kept by Adolf Eichmann, an SS officer and Heydrich's assistant.

Eichmann presented a listing of the Jews living in areas occupied by the Germans or allied to them. The list was extensive, ranging from 5,000,000 in Russia and 2,284,000 in Poland, to 1,300 in Norway and 200 in Albania. At the bottom, Eichmann typed: "Total: over 11,000,000."

Using euphemisms like "final solution", the bureaucrats at Wannsee discussed the details of identifying, transporting and killing eleven million people. They talked about how to define a Jew (having two Jewish grandparents was enough), how to organize the railways to carry so many people, how to select those who could be worked to death and those who were to be killed immediately, whether gassing was the most efficient means of mass murder, and how to dispose of so many human remains. Then they broke for snacks, gossiped, got in their cars and went home. Evil men are not always raging killers; sometimes they can be mild-mannered clerks worried about train timetables.

PQ 17

The escorts and merchant ships before the sailing of PQ 17

In 1942, the ongoing struggle to ferry supplies across the Atlantic from Canada to keep beleaguered Britain alive continued, but it was not the only important convoy route. The Russians had lost huge amounts of equipment in the first months of their war against Germany, and every tank, gun or jeep they could get would help in their battles in besieged Leningrad and outside Moscow.

Unfortunately, the only route a convoy could take to Russia year round was around the top of Norway and Sweden to the ice-free port of Murmansk. This meant both sailing in atrocious conditions and travelling close to German occupied territory. While the sailors fought to prevent their ships capsizing from the weight of ice building up on their decks, they were attacked by submarines, aircraft and surface raiders.

Convoy PQ 17 was the largest to date when it sailed from Iceland on June 27, 1942. Thirty-five ships carried $700 million worth of trucks, jeeps, tanks, bombers and supplies. It was protected by a large escort of destroyers and corvettes.

PQ 17 was sighted by the enemy on July 1, and the first two ships were sunk on July 4. The next day, based on a report that German battleships were on their way to attack, the convoy was ordered to disperse and the ships to make their own way to Murmansk. Over the next six days, a further twenty-one ships were sunk by bombers or submarines. The following cargo disappeared into the Arctic Ocean: 3330 tanks, 200 bombers, 93316 tones of cargo, and 153 drowned in the frigid waters. Two more vessels were sunk on the way home.

A torpedoed merchant ship

PQ 18 didn't sail until September, and it still lost thirteen ships. After that, the Murmansk convoys sailed in the protective darkness of winter.

War At Home

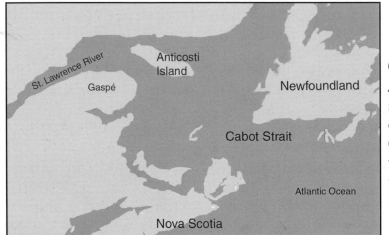

On the opposite side of the Atlantic from PQ 17, the summer of 1942 saw the war come home to parts of Canada. On June 10, a U-boat sank two freighters off Anticosti Island in the mouth of the St. Lawrence River.

For the rest of the summer, the inhabitants of the Gaspé coast and along the shores of the St. Lawrence River and Gulf became used to explosions rattling their windows and bodies and debris drifting onto their beaches. The worst attack happened on the night of October 14, when the passenger ferry *SS Caribou* was torpedoed in Cabot Strait. One hundred and thirty-seven passengers and crew died.

Pressure mounted for the Canadian government to reduce help to the Atlantic convoys and bring ships back to the St. Lawrence. Canada did not; the lifeline to Britain was too vital.

Caribou

Crisis in Canada

Canadian wartime prime minister
William Lyon Mackenzie King

An anti-conscription rally
in Quebec

In WW I, conscription (forcing young men to join the army and fight) was tremendously unpopular across Canada. In 1940, not wanting a repeat of the WW I crisis, Prime Minister King introduced conscription, but only for service within Canada. If you didn't volunteer, you wouldn't have to go and fight.

In 1942, the government held a plebiscite asking voters to accept a reversal of that policy. In English Canada, 83% voted yes. In Quebec, 72.9% voted no. The government changed the bill of 1940 to allow overseas service for conscripts. There were some protests but, as no one was immediately sent overseas, the issue died down.

However, by 1944, Canada was short of soldiers, and the prime minister ordered a one-time levy of 17,000 conscripts to be sent overseas. This triggered the most serious mutiny in Canadian military history.

When news reached the conscripts of the 15th Canadian Infantry Brigade in Terrace, B.C. on November 24, 1944, they refused to obey their officers. Some soldiers seized weapons and were prepared to resist attempts to force them overseas.

Major General George Pearkes, who had won a Victoria Cross at Passchendaele during WW I, managed to defuse the situation, although he was critical of the government's poor handling of the situation. By November 29th, all was quiet again.

In fact, by the end of the war, fewer than three thousand conscripted men had reached the front lines. Seventy-nine of them were killed.

Battles without Seeing the Enemy

The American fleet didn't have it entirely its own way at Midway. Early on June 4, fifteen Douglas Devastator torpedo bombers were launched from the USS *Hornet* against the Japanese carriers.

Already outdated in 1942, the Devastators had no protection from the fast Japanese Zero fighters. Every American plane was shot down without inflicting any damage. Of the thirty crew members, only one man, Ensign George Gay, survived. For thirty hours, Gay floated in the Pacific, watching subsequent American attacks sink three Japanese carriers, before he was rescued. Devastators were not used offensively again.

By the spring of 1942, Japan controlled Malaya, Singapore, Thailand, Burma, the Philippines and numerous important islands in the eastern Pacific. Its objective was to create a large enough empire that Japan itself would be safe from attack. In May, they sent an invasion force toward Port Moresby in New Guinea, from where they could threaten Australia.

Unfortunately for the Japanese, the Americans could read their naval code and were waiting in the Coral Sea. The ensuing battle was fought without the major ships of either side seeing or firing on each other. However, Japanese planes sank the carrier *Lexington* and damaged the *Yorktown.* The Japanese fleet lost only one small carrier, so it could count the battle a victory. However, they had to call off their invasion of New Guinea.

The Battle of the Coral Sea marked the first time a Japanese invasion had been foiled. The Japanese realized that the problem was the American carriers that had escaped the attack on Pearl Harbor. Exactly a month after the Coral Sea battle, they tried to remedy that.

The Japanese attack on Midway Island, at the extreme northwestern end of the

Midway atoll

A Japanese
aircraft carrier

Hawaiian Island chain, was designed to draw the remaining American carriers into a decisive battle. As at the Coral Sea, the Americans were reading the Japanese coded messages and were ready.

Between June 4 and 7, the Japanese lost four carriers and one cruiser was sunk, 332 aircraft were destroyed and hundreds of trained pilots killed. The Americans lost only one carrier, the *Yorktown* (which had been rushed through repairs after the Coral Sea), a destroyer and 98 aircraft.

Midway crippled the Japanese fleet. It took them until 1945 to replace the lost carriers and they never managed to replace the experienced pilots. By 1945, the Americans had commissioned over two dozen new carriers and trained hundreds of pilots.

The Japanese battle cruiser
Mikumi sinking

Practice

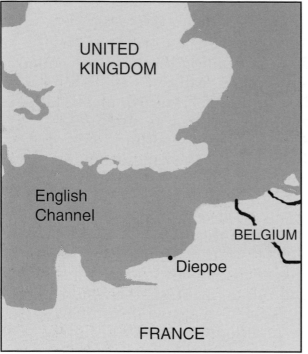

The English Channel is like a vast medieval moat around a castle. Without it, Rommel's and Guderian's Panzers would have rolled north through the English countryside in 1940. But by 1942, Britain was safe and the Channel presented a problem in the opposite direction.

If Europe was ever to be freed from Nazi domination, a huge army would have to fight its way through France and into the German heartland. Already, Stalin was demanding the invasion of France to help take the pressure off his strained armies in Russia. With America in the war, the Allies would soon have the armies, but how to get them into France without them being slaughtered on the beaches?

It might be possible to capture a major port and use that to feed men, machines and supplies to an Allied army on French soil. In 1942, the job of seeing if this were possible was given to the Canadian 2nd Division. The port chosen was Dieppe.

On the morning of August 19, more than six thousand Canadians, supported by hundreds of ships and

Canadian dead on the beach at Dieppe

36

Louis Mountbatten, whose idea Dieppe had been, said, "the Battle of Normandy was won on the beaches of Dieppe. For every man who died in Dieppe at least ten more must have been spared in Normandy in 1944."

planes, stormed ashore up the gravel beaches of Dieppe and the flanking towns of Puys and Pourville. By lunchtime, 3,367 were either dead, wounded or prisoners, and the rest were heading back to Britain. Abandoned tanks, armoured cars and burning landing craft littered the beach, and 119 aircraft had been shot out of the sky. The German defenders suffered 311 killed, wounded or missing and lost 46 planes.

The Germans were few but well placed. For example, at Puys, the 622 men of the Royal Canadian Regiment who made it ashore were faced by only 60 defenders. Despite this, 225 Canadians were killed, 264 taken prisoner and only 33 made it back to England.

The raid on Dieppe was a disaster, but lessons were learned.

Canadian POWs in German captivity after Dieppe

Turning Tides

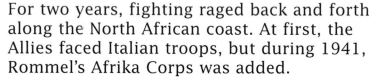

El Alamein • • Alexandria

LIBYA

• Cairo

EGYPT

General Montgomery

For two years, fighting raged back and forth along the North African coast. At first, the Allies faced Italian troops, but during 1941, Rommel's Afrika Corps was added.

Rommel's experience in France and the ideal nature of the desert for tank warfare overwhelmed the Allies, and by July 1942, they had been pushed back to the town of El Alamein, only a hundred kilometres from Alexandria.

If Rommel broke into Egypt, closed the Suez Canal to British ships and took control of the Middle Eastern oil fields, it would be a major victory for the Axis. Fortunately, Rommel, short of supplies, couldn't break through the British defences. The two sides sat looking at each other and resupplying.

In August, Churchill placed General Bernard Montgomery in charge. His first task was to stop another Axis offensive in August, but by October he was ready to go on the offensive.

The Second Battle of El Alamein lasted from October 23 to November 5. The fighting was ferocious, with tens of thousands of casualties and hundreds of tanks and guns lost on both sides. But the British could replace their losses; Rommel could not and, with only some twenty tanks left, he disobeyed Hitler's order to fight to the last man and withdrew.

After the war, Churchill said that before El Alamein, the Allies never won a battle, after it they never lost one.

El Alamein was a turning point in the war and, like Midway in the Pacific, a desperately needed boost to Allied morale. As Churchill said only days after the battle, "...this is not the end. It is not even the beginning of the end. But it is, perhaps, the end of the beginning."

Churchill was a master of the ringing phrase, but the war against Germany would not be won in either North Africa or the Pacific Ocean. Even as he was speaking about endings and beginnings, there was a battle raging in the Russian city of Stalingrad that would prove to be the biggest turning point of all.

On November 8, using something of what had been learned at Dieppe, Allied forces landed at Casablanca, Oran and Algiers at the western end of North Africa. Rommel was now trapped. On May 13, 1943, all remaining Axis forces in Africa surrendered. The Allies now had a base from which to attack Sicily, Italy and southern Europe.

British tanks at El Alamein

Stalingrad

It was not only Russian soldiers that fought at Stalingrad. Civilian women and children, who were not allowed to leave the city, dug trenches, and factory workers drove newly built unpainted tanks into battle.

The fighters were not only men. Female snipers became famous, and untrained girls manned anti-aircraft guns and fought tanks until all were killed.

For months, Stalingrad was a place where only fighting and death ruled. It was total war on a scale the world had never seen before.

Soviet soldiers in the ruins of Stalingrad

Wolfram Freiherr von Richthofen was a distant cousin of the WW I flying ace, the Red Baron. He had learned his craft in planning Guernica and perfected it over Warsaw and during Operation Barbarossa. On August 23, 1942, he launched the bombers of Luftflotte 4 against the Russian city of Stalingrad and opened the bloodiest battle in human history.

After the Barbarossa campaign had failed to defeat Russia in 1941, Hitler decided to concentrate in 1942 on taking the Caucasus oilfields and the industrial city of Stalingrad on the Volga River.

At first it was like the days of 1941 as the Panzers raced across the open Russian Steppes. By the end of August, they had reached the Volga on both sides of Stalingrad, meaning that the only supplies into the beleaguered city had to come over the heavily bombed river.

Luftflotte 4's attacks turned Stalingrad into a city of rubble and killed thousands. They also made it an ideal place to defend. Small groups of Russian soldiers held onto ruined buildings for days as General Friedrich Paulus's 6th Army, the Army that the Canadians had fought at Vimy Ridge in 1917, struggled to take the city.

The fighting in Stalingrad was brutal.

Russian soldiers
in the rubble

To neutralize the German advantages in artillery and bombers, the Russian soldiers fought so close to their enemy that any German supporting fire would kill as many of their own solders as their opponents. The Russians also shot any of their own men who retreated and, at one stage, the average life expectancy of a young Russian soldier being thrown over the Volga into the battle was twenty-four hours.

The highest spot in downtown Stalingrad, now called Volgograd is a hill called Mamayev Kurgan. It and the area around it were fought over so many times that of the 10,000 original members of the Russian 13th Guards Rifle Division, only 320 survived the entire battle.

The Germans called the fighting Rattenkrieg or Rat War and joked that you could capture the kitchen of a house and still have to fight for the living room. One apartment building was fought over for two months, and the Russians claimed that the Germans lost more men taking it than they had in taking Paris.

As the weather got colder, the Germans inched through the city. By late November, the Russians held only a narrow strip along the river, in some places a mere few tens of metres wide. But the tide was about to turn.

Russian Victory

Stalingrad was at the eastern end of a wide bulge in the German lines. The flanks of this bulge were held by weak, poorly-equipped Romanian and Croatian troops. On November 19, in a thick fog, three Russian armies smashed through the northern flank. The following day, two more armies attacked from the south. On November 22, the Russian armies met at the town of Kalach, trapping 290,000 men, mostly of Paulus's 6th Army, in and around Stalingrad.

Because Stalingrad was named for the Russian dictator, the battle there became a symbol—Stalin could not afford to lose it, and Hitler was desperate to hold it. Paulus and the 6th Army were ordered to hold their ground and not try to break out of the trap. An attack aimed at relieving the 6th Army failed and Russian attacks in the south forced the rest of the German armies further and further from their beleaguered comrades. Attempts to supply the 6th Army from the air also failed.

A Russian propaganda poster

It was quite common in Communist countries for the regime to rename towns after its famous leaders:

St. Petersburg/Petrograd = Leningrad
Volgograd = Stalingrad
Saigon = Ho Chi Minh City (Vietnam)
Chemnitz = Karl-Marx-Stadt (East Germany)

As the winter dragged on, the Germans ran out of supplies. Under constant attack, the soldiers now had to contend with frostbite, malnutrition and starvation. Finally, on February 2, Paulus, 22 generals and 91,000 sick and starving survivors surrendered. Only about 5,000 of these survived the Russian labour camps, and the last of them was repatriated to Germany in 1955.

The Battle of Stalingrad lasted 199 days and cost almost two million casualties. After the battle, the German army fought fiercely, but never recovered the strength it had before. The Russian army grew from strength to strength. Stalingrad truly was the beginning of the end for Germany.

A soldier celebrates Russian victory

Technology

The close of 1942 saw the Allies in a much better position than they had been a year before. Japanese expansion had been stopped at the Coral Sea and Midway, the Nazis at El Alamein and Stalingrad.

The industrial might and huge populations of America and Russia were beginning to produce planes, tanks, ships, weapons, trucks and trained soldiers, sailors and airmen in quantities that the Japanese, Germans and Italians could not match. Technological advances were pointing to a future that few could even imagine.

The Me 262 jet plane

Wars are always times when technology takes a leap forward. Unfortunately, developments are usually in better ways to kill people. WW I, for example, gave the world poison gas and the tanks and planes that would become the major tools of WW II.

Throughout the 1930s, German research led the world in many fields. As a

This is an image of the first ever nuclear explosion a fraction of a second after detonation. It was the result of the work of Oppenheimer and his colleagues.

result, the German forces began the war in 1939 with more efficient weapons (although British, French and Russian tanks were generally superior in 1940 and 1941). German technology fell behind for two reasons. Many Jewish scientists fled Nazi anti-semitism in the thirties, and Hitler, expecting a short war, did not put money into research and development.

Despite this, two of the major innovations of WW II were German. On July 18, 1942, the world's first jet plane, the Me 262, flew at the air base at Leipheim. On October 3 of the same year, at Peenemunde, a V2 rocket became the first man-made object to reach space.

Fortunately for the Allies, both these innovations came too late to affect the war. What did have an effect was a conference at Berkeley in California in the summer of 1942. Physicist J. Robert Oppenheimer led the top scientists of his day in a study of whether it would be possible to build a huge bomb using nuclear fission. They determined that it was theoretically possible, and the nuclear age was born.

Resistance

"We will not be silent."
-The White Rose

Captured French
resistance members

Despite El Alamein and Stalingrad, 1943 saw the Nazis solidly in control of Europe. Nonetheless, they still faced resistance in the territories they had occupied.

Most occupied countries resisted in some way. The vast areas of Russia overrun by the Germans contained thousands of well-organized partisans who, despite brutal reprisals, caused major disruptions to German supply lines and communications. In France, resistance groups, organized and supplied from Britain, spied and prepared for the inevitable invasion. In Denmark, all but 450 of the country's 8,000 Jews were ferried over to safety in neutral Sweden by the resistance before the Germans could deport them to concentration camps.

It is natural for people to resist invaders, but was there resistance to Hitler and the Nazis within Germany?

The German socialists and communists who had fought the Nazis in the streets in the early thirties were, by the 1940s, dead, in exile or in concentration camps. Although the organized religions did little to oppose Hitler, a few brave men spoke out. Dietrich

Sophie Scholl's final words were, "Such a fine, sunny day, and I have to leave. But what does my death matter, if through us thousands of people are awakened and stirred to action?"

The Scholls believed that their leaflets would inspire or guilt Germans into resisting the Nazis. In their second leaflet they said, "Since the conquest of Poland three hundred thousand Jews have been murdered in this country in the most bestial way… The German people slumber on in their dull, stupid sleep and encourage these fascist criminals… Each man…is guilty, guilty, guilty!"

The White Rose's efforts had little effect, but the Scholls and the others have become heroes since. There are squares named after them in Germany, movies made about them, and the young readers of a German magazine voted Sophie Scholl the greatest woman of the twentieth century. The White Rose statement, "We will not be silent" has become an international T-shirt slogan opposing the war in Iraq.

Lillian Garrett-Groag, who wrote a play about the White Rose, said, "The fact that five little kids, in the mouth of the wolf, where it really counted, had the tremendous courage to do what they did, is spectacular to me. I know that the world is better for them having been there."

Bonhoeffer, a Protestant pastor, was arrested in April 1943 for being involved in a plot to assassinate Hitler. He was executed a month before the war ended.

The Nazis not only cracked down on violent resistance. Between June, 1942 and February, 1943, a group of students from the University of Munich and their philosophy professor printed and distributed six leaflets criticizing the Nazis. The were led by Hans and Sophie Scholl, two students in their early twenties, who called themselves the White Rose. For this non-violent resistance, the Scholls and others of the White Rose were arrested, tried and beheaded.

A German postage stamp commemorating Sophie Scholl's short, brave life

Holocaust

Evidence of genocide: eyeglasses confiscated from victims

Although they formed the majority of the victims, it was not only Jews who died in the Holocaust. The Nazis slaughtered or worked to death some two to three million Russian prisoners of war, almost half a million Romani (known then as Gypsies), 250,000 disabled people, 80,000 to 200,000 Freemasons, 5,000 to 15,000 homosexuals and between 2,500 and 5,000 Jehovah's Witnesses. If you want to read their names as well, it will take you grades 10 and 11 too.

If, instead of learning things in school, you spent every minute of every class reading the names of the six million Jewish men, women and children who were murdered by the Nazis in WW II, it would take you all of grades 7, 8 and 9.

By the time Heydrich and Eichmann sat down at Wannsee in January 1942, over one million Jews had already been killed. They had been shot on the edges of deep pits or sealed in vans filled with carbon monoxide gas from the van's engine. But even this was not enough horror for Himmler and his SS.

From the beginning of their rule, the Nazis had built concentration camps to house those they considered dangerous or undesirable. Eventually, many of these became labour camps where socialists, communists, criminals and Russian prisoners of war were worked to death. They were terrible places where death was commonplace, but there were camps that were much worse.

The systematic murder of most of Europe's Jews took place in six extermination camps. Three, Majdenek, Chelmno and Auschwitz-Birkenau, already existed and three, Belzec, Sobibor and Treblinka, were specially built.

The tentacles of Himmler's "Final Solution" reached along the railway lines throughout Europe. Throughout the war, Jews from Poland, Germany, Russia, the Ukraine, Greece,

Starving inmates liberated at Buchenwald. The group includes future acclaimed author Elie Wiesel.

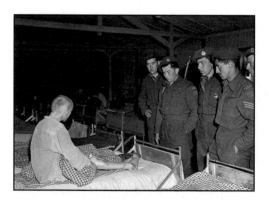

Sombre Canadian liberators with a malnourished Holocaust victim

France, the Netherlands, Hungary, Italy, Slovakia, Belgium, Romania and a host of other countries were packed into cattle cars and sent either directly to one of the extermination centres, or into a ghetto in a major city to await their turn.

On arrival at a death camp, the victims were hurried to a concrete building, where, they were often told, they were to be disinfected. Women had their heads shaved, and everyone was told to undress and leave their possessions in a pile. They were then crammed into the buildings, the doors were sealed, and gas, either cyanide or exhaust fumes from a large engine, was pumped in until everyone was dead. The bodies were then either buried or burned. In this way, 800,000 men, women and children died at Treblinka alone.

The victim's valuables, including gold teeth, clothing, shoes and eyeglasses, were taken. Their hair was used for bedding in submarines because human hair does not absorb moisture.

It is hard to imagine how some people can do such things to others. Even if you are being told that the victims are less than human, how can you kill a child? And yet it was done.

Perhaps the most chilling comment on the Holocaust was made by Franz Stangl, the commandant at Treblinka. He was finally arrested in Brazil in 1967 and tried for mass murder. He did not deny the horrors he had overseen but said, "My conscience is clear. I was simply doing my duty."

Going Quietly?

For many of the doomed of the Holocaust, it was important that the world know what was going on. Records were buried in the camps, and the ghettos, and people escaped so they could carry the news back to other Jews and a disbelieving outside world. Survivors wrote and talked of their experiences in order to bear witness to the horror that they had lived through.

Did six million Jews walk quietly to their doom in the gas chambers of Treblinka and Auschwitz?

Many did because they couldn't imagine the scale of the horror they were a part of, or because they believed the stories of being disinfected, or because they had simply given up hope. But there were also countless cases of individual resistance ranging from hopeless attacks on guards to escape attempts in an attempt to tell the world what was going on. There were also large revolts.

Thousands of Jews fought as partisans in the forests of the Ukraine, Poland and Russia. Even within the death camps there was resistance. A "Sonderkommando" unit, prisoners who were forced to dispose of the bodies before they themselves were killed, revolted at Auschwitz, and inmates at both Sobibor and Treblinka rebelled, killed SS guards and escaped into the surrounding forests. About fifty people from each of those camps survived the war to tell the world. In contrast, only two people survived from the half a million who died at Belzec and, consequently, that camp is not nearly so well known.

Female partisans captured in the Warsaw ghetto

Simon Wiesenthal, a Polish architect from Lvov, survived twelve different camps, although the almost six foot tall man weighed a mere 99 pounds on his release in 1945. Having lost 89 relatives in the Holocaust, Wiesenthal devoted much of his life to finding and bringing to justice those who had carried out the horrors. He and the organization he founded were instrumental in bringing dozens of camp guards and organizers to trial, including Heydrich's assistant Adolf Eichmann and Franz Stangl, the commandant at both Treblinka and Sobibor.

Wiesenthal believed that it was important to try the guilty from the Holocaust, not only for justice, but also to make sure that people would remember the horrors. Wiesenthal died peacefully in his sleep at the age of 96 on September 20, 2005.

The largest uprising happened in the Warsaw ghetto, where hundreds of thousands of Jews were collected before being sent onto the Treblinka camp. On January 18, 1943, German troops entering the ghetto to round up the next shipment to the death camps were met with a hail of small arms fire and the explosions of homemade bombs. The deportation was cancelled.

Through April and May, SS troops battled Jewish fighters through the ruins of the ghetto. The fighters were doomed, but they fought on, taking to the sewers when the buildings above were burned and dynamited. Ultimately, the last of the ghetto inhabitants was sent to Treblinka and killed, but they did not go quietly.

The building of the wall to enclose the Warsaw ghetto

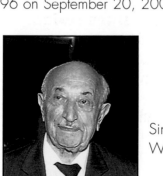

Simon Wiesenthal

51

Hiding

All across Europe, even in Berlin itself, tens of thousands of Jews, many of them children separated from their parents, attempted to hide from the machinery of the Holocaust. Children who did not look Jewish were taken in by non-Jewish families. Others were sheltered by nuns and priests or took shelter in cellars or hidden rooms. Some businessmen, such as Oskar Schindler, protected their Jewish workers through bribery.

Hiding Jews could be hazardous. In Poland, where the penalty for sheltering a Jew was death, the reward for turning a hidden Jew in to the Nazis was a bottle of vodka and a hundred cigarettes.

Although thousands of individuals risked their lives to save thousands of Jews, the most famous case was a failure.

Anne Frank's family fled Germany to what they thought was the safety of the Netherlands in 1933. In July, 1942, when Anne had just turned 13, her family went into

Anne Frank

Anne's father survived Auschwitz and returned to the Netherlands to find that Anne's diary had survived. He had it published, and it has become one of the best known and most moving documents of the Holocaust. Simon Wiesenthal said that Anne's diary had done more to raise awareness of the Holocaust than the post-war trials at Nuremberg.

Anne is often put forward as a symbol of the suffering and horror of the Holocaust. However, as Miep Gies, one of those who supplied the Franks with food, said, "Anne's life and death were her own individual fate, an individual fate that happened six million times over... Her fate helps us grasp the immense loss the world suffered because of the Holocaust."

hiding in a secret room. For two years, they and another family were supplied with food and necessities by loyal employees. During those two years, Anne kept a diary.

The diary of Anne Frank records a teenage girl's day-to-day frustrations at being cooped up for so long with so many others. She talks about her life, her relationships with the others and her hopes for the future.

But there was to be no future for Anne. In the summer of 1944, someone, whose identity has never been established, betrayed the secret annex, and all in it were arrested.

Anne's mother died in Auschwitz, and Anne and her sister Margot died of typhus in Bergen-Belsen camp in March, 1945, mere weeks before it was liberated.

A statue of Anne Frank in Amsterdam. There are memorials and tributes to her around the world.

A Poetic War?

Theresienstadt was an Austrian fortress where Gavrilo Princip, the man who shot Archduke Franz Ferdinand to trigger WW I, was held before he died in cell #1. In WW II the Germans turned it into a concentration camp. Over fourteen thousand children died at Theresienstadt, but some of the poems they wrote survived. It is not known who wrote this one:

On a Sunny Evening

On a purple, sun-shot evening,
Under wide-flowering chestnut trees,
Upon the threshold full of dust,
Yesterday, today, the days are all like these.
Trees flower forth in beauty,
Lovely too their very wood all gnarled and old,
That I am half afraid to peer
Into their crowns of green and gold.
The sun has made a veil of gold,
So lovely that my body aches,
Above, the heavens shriek with blue.
Convinced I've smiled by some mistake,
The world's abloom and seems to smile.
I want to fly but where, how high,
If in barbed wire, things can bloom.
Why couldn't I? I will not die!

The poetry and poets from WW I are much better known than from WW II. Everyone knows at least some of John McCrae's "In Flanders Fields". Perhaps the most famous WW II poem is Randall Jarrell's "The Death of the Ball Turret Gunner":

From my mother's sleep I fell into the State,
And I hunched in its belly till my wet fur froze.
Six miles from earth, loosed
from its dream of life,
I woke to black flak and the nightmare fighters.
When I died they washed me out of the turret
with a hose.

Because WW II was truly a world war, there was much poetry written elsewhere in other languages. For example, in 1941, before he went off to war, Russian author Konstantin Simonov wrote "To Valentina Serova" for his girlfriend.

Simonov

Wait for me, and I'll come back!
Wait with all you've got!
Wait, when dreary yellow rains
Tell you, you should not.
Wait when snow is falling fast,
Wait when summer's hot,
Wait when yesterdays are past,
Others are forgot.
Wait, when from that far-off place,
Letters don't arrive.
Wait, when those with whom you wait
Doubt if I'm alive...
Wait for me and I'll come back,
Dodging every fate!
"What a bit of luck!" they'll say,
Those that would not wait.
They will never understand
How amidst the strife,
By your waiting for me, dear,
You had saved my life.
Only you and I will know
How you got me through.
Simply—you knew how to wait—
No one else but you.

Simonov survived the war and returned to
marry Valentina.

General Patton with
Britain's Louis Mountbatten

General George S. Patton was in
command of the American troops in
Sicily. He was an excellent and
aggressive leader, but he was
involved in two controversial incidents.

In two separate incidents, American
troops shot 74 Italian and 2 German
prisoners of war. An American
sergeant was stripped of his rank and
imprisoned and a captain tried and
acquitted. They claimed to be
following orders, specifically Patton's
speech before the invasion when he
told his men that even if the enemy
tried to surrender, they should be shot.

On a visit to a hospital, Patton was
introduced to a soldier probably suffering
from post-traumatic stress disorder. The
general swore at the soldier and hit him.
Patton later apologized, but he was
relieved of his command.

Taking it Back

The Allies took the offensive in 1943.

In the Pacific, the Americans began the long
and bloody process of "island-hopping"
toward the Japanese homeland. In Russia, the
Red Army pushed the Germans back, and at
Kursk, the largest tank battle in history,
destroyed hundreds of irreplaceable German
tanks and planes. In Europe, the Allies moved
from North Africa to Sicily and Italy.

At dawn on July 10, 1943, more than twenty
thousand men of the 1st Canadian Infantry
Division and the First Canadian Army Tank
Brigade stormed up the beaches around
Pachino in southern Sicily. They were part of a
British and American force whose job was to
take the island in preparation for the invasion
of the Italian mainland.

After the disasters at Hong Kong and Dieppe,
the Canadians were eager to prove themselves,
but it was not easy. As the Allies advanced across
the island, the Canadians had to fight in rugged,
trackless terrain, battling for every rocky hilltop.
It took four attacks and five days to take the
village of Agira alone.

In 27 days of fighting, the Canadians advanced
240 kilometres at a cost of 562 killed and 1,848
wounded or taken prisoner. The way to Italy was
now open.

Conferences

Stalin dominated the Tehran Conference. Roosevelt was unwell and didn't support Churchill, whereas Stalin was jubilant after the huge Russian victories at Stalingrad and Kursk.

Throughout the conference, Stalin needled Churchill about being "soft" on Germany. At the dinner, Stalin proposed executing 50,000 German officers after the war. Churchill was horrified at what he considered the "cold blooded execution of soldiers who fought for their country." Roosevelt defused the situation by jokingly suggesting that perhaps only 49,000 executions would do.

What Roosevelt didn't realize was that Stalin probably wasn't joking. Already in 1940, he had approved the massacre of some 22,000 Polish officers, prisoners of war and intellectuals in the forest of Katyn. The mass graves had been discovered by the Nazis, but the Americans and British refused to publicly believe the evidence for fear of upsetting their Russian ally.

The complexity of several major allies fighting a long war required numerous conferences to discuss overall strategy.

Roosevelt and Churchill met several times in Washington, Casablanca and Quebec, but the three Allied leaders, Roosevelt, Churchill and Stalin, met for the first time at Tehran, in Iran, in November and December 1943. There they decided that the cross-channel invasion of France would take priority and be attempted in June of 1944. They also agreed on the independence of Iran and Korea and the establishment of a United Nations organization after the war.

The three only met once more, at Yalta, in Ukraine, in February, 1945, but Roosevelt's successor, Harry Truman, met with Churchill and Stalin at Potsdam, outside Berlin, in July and August of that year.

Churchill, Roosevelt and Stalin at Yalta

Last Gasps

In the twelfth century, Mongolian invasion fleets bound for Japan were destroyed by storms. The Japanese thought the storms were sent by the gods and called them divine wind, or Kamikaze. As WW II turned against Japan, the divine wind was resurrected in a terrible form.

At 10:51 on the morning of October 25, during the Battle of Leyte Gulf, a Zero fighter deliberately crashed into a carrier, the *St. Lo*. It exploded and sank, becoming the first victim of the Kamikaze suicide attacks.

Some young Japanese pilots considered it an honour to volunteer for Kamikaze suicide missions, but many were forced to fly them after long and extremely brutal training.

Over the last ten months of the war, almost three thousand Kamikaze attacks sank about fifty vessels.

Young women see off a Kamikaze pilot

In March 1944, Japanese troops swept over the Chindwin River into India. Encouraged by unrest at British rule in India and by Indian nationalists fighting beside them, the Japanese expected easy victories like those of 1941 and 1942.

The Japanese surrounded and laid siege to the town of Imphal, but lack of air support, tanks and supplies doomed their attack. By July, the ragged, starving remnants of the Japanese invasion were being pursued back into Burma. With 55,000 casualties, it was the largest defeat the Japanese had suffered.

In June, while the British were pushing the Japanese out of India, to the east the largest carrier battle in history was unfolding.

As the Americans island-hopped through the Mariana Islands, the Japanese navy tried to stop them. The result, on June 19 and 20, was what the American pilots called the "Marianas Turkey Shoot". Three Japanese carriers were sunk, two by submarines, and some six thousand planes destroyed.

The Japanese lost so much that at the Battle of Leyte Gulf in October, they could only use their remaining carriers as decoys, since they did not have enough planes to equip them.

After the loss of four more carriers, nine battleships and twenty cruisers at Leyte Gulf, the Japanese navy effectively ceased to exist. Nothing was left to stop the Americans moving inexorably closer to Japan itself.

Italy

Three Canadians won Victoria Crosses in Italy.

On December 14, 1943, near Ortona, Captain Paul Triquet led his men on a wild charge into the outskirts of Casa Berardi and held on until relieved.

In May, 1944, Major John Mahony, despite being wounded in the head and leg, led his men in a heroic defence of a bridgehead over the River Melfa.

In October, 1944, Private Ernest (Smokey) Smith destroyed a German tank and, when charged by ten enemy soldiers, jumped out in front of them, firing his gun at point-blank range, killing four and driving the rest off.

Less than a month after the last Axis soldier left Sicily, British, American and Canadian troops landed on mainland Italy. Almost immediately, the Italians declared an armistice and stopped fighting, but the Germans established a series of defensive lines south of Rome.

By November, 1943, the Allies had reached the Gustav Line running right across Italy, over 100 kilometres south of Rome. The eastern end of the line was anchored on the Adriatic port of Ortona.

For eight days in December, the Loyal Edmonton Regiment and the Seaforth Highlanders of Canada, later supported by the Princess Patricia's Canadian Light Infantry and tanks from the 1st Canadian Armoured Brigade, fought in the streets of Ortona, in what came to be known as the Canadian Stalingrad.

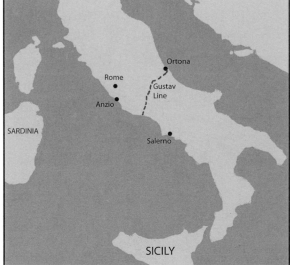

A German soldier surrenders to Canadians in Ortona.

Allied soldiers on the
Anzio beachhead

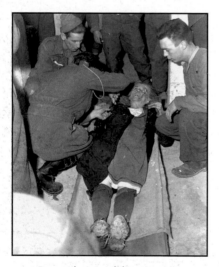

Canadian soldiers assist
a wounded Italian woman.

A Canadian at the grave
of an Italian soldier

The German defenders of Ortona deliberately demolished the town and set up defences in the rubble, including mines, booby traps and tanks buried so that only their turret showed. Since moving through the deadly streets was so difficult, the Canadians resorted to a technique called mouse-holing.

Mouse-holing involved blowing holes in the walls of buildings and moving from room to room. Often the Canadians had to fight at close quarters from room to room in individual houses. By the time Ortona was cleared, Canada had suffered some six hundred casualties.

After Ortona fell, attention focussed on the west. In January, landings by British and American troops at Anzio, less than forty kilometres from Rome, became bogged down with heavy casualties, including the father of rock band Pink Floyd's Roger Waters.

To break through the Gustav line to Anzio and Rome required taking the hilltop monastery of Monte Cassino. Between January and May, 1944, American, British, New

Zealand, French, South African, Canadian and Polish troops fought four battles in the ruins. Eventually, the monastery fell and, on June 5, the Americans entered Rome.

Not all bombing of cities was by hundreds of planes. On February 18, 1944, nineteen Mosquito bombers carried out a precision raid on the prison at Amiens. The object of the raid was to release French Resistance fighters, many of whom were scheduled for execution the following day.

Flying at high speed at rooftop height along Amiens' streets, the Mosquitos dropped 500-pound bombs onto the prison, destroying walls and the guards' barracks. One hundred prisoners were killed in the raid, but 258 escaped, including a man who knew the vital secrets of Operation Overlord, the Allied plan to invade Europe.

Guernica's Legacy

In the early days of WW II, the only way Britain could hit back at Germany was by using long-range bombers. To be relatively safe, the bombers had to bomb either at night or from very high altitude during the day, and the technology didn't exist to do that accurately.

The answer was to target a large area, like a city. On May 30, 1942, over a thousand bombers attacked Cologne, setting the city on fire, leaving thousands homeless and hundreds dead.

Over eight days in July a year later, the British attacked Hamburg by night while the Americans bombed by day. On the night of July 27, the bombing created a firestorm. A firestorm is a single city-wide blaze reaching temperatures of 800° Celsius and creating winds of 240 kilometres per hour. The firestorm in Hamburg killed over forty thousand people and left almost a million homeless.

Other German cities, Darmstadt, Kassel and Dresden suffered a similar fate, but it was the wooden Japanese cities that were most susceptible. On the night of March 9-10, 1945, forty-one square kilometres of Tokyo burned, and a hundred thousand people died.

The ruins of downtown Hamburg after the firestorm

Tokyo aflame

Canada was not bombed in WW II but made a significant contribution to the campaign in Europe. Sixteen thousand bombers were built in Canada, and 130,000 aircrew members were trained. Thirteen thousand Royal Canadian Air Force (R.C.A.F.) personnel were killed in the war.

In addition to fighting, Canada supplied over seventeen thousand members of the R.C.A.F. Women's Division, whose jobs included ferrying the new bombers from Canada to wherever they were needed.

The devastation of Dresden's core after Allied bombing

A woman in the uniform of the R.C.A.F. women's division

D-Day

By the summer of 1944, everyone knew that the invasion of France was imminent. But when and where?

When was the easier question, since a successful landing required a full moon, high tides and good weather. The Allies expended a vast amount of energy and resources on disguising where.

The most obvious place to cross the channel was at Calais, the narrowest point. As D-Day approached, the French Resistance was active near Calais, radio messages were increased, fake concentrations of equipment were concentrated in southeast England, and troops were marched around to give the impression of a large invasion preparation.

At a reception in London, General Patton shouted loudly across the room to another officer that he would see him soon in Calais. People were shocked at Patton's blunder, but it was a setup, another part of the plan to convince the Germans to defend the wrong part of the coast.

Operation Overlord, which began on June 6, 1944, D-Day, was the largest amphibious invasion of all time. In one day, 130,000 troops landed on enemy soil. They arrived by parachute, glider and landing craft on five beaches along the Normandy coast of occupied France.

The Americans landed on two beaches, Utah and Omaha, the British on two, Gold and Sword, and the Canadians on one, Juno. All five landings were successful, although the landing on Omaha beach, recreated in the movie, *Saving Private Ryan*, only succeeded at great cost.

At 7:45 a.m., the first soldiers of the 3rd Canadian Infantry Division splashed ashore at Juno beach. They were met by strong defences, and in the first hour suffered fifty per cent casualties, similar to those suffered by the Americans on Omaha. However, once the beaches were secured, the Canadians moved rapidly inland and ended the day deeper in enemy territory than any other landing force.

Total Allied casualties were around ten thousand, mostly American. Three hundred and forty Canadians died that day but, by sundown, a solid foothold had been gained. The lessons of Dieppe had been learned, and the Allies were back in France in force.

Caen and Falaise

D-Day plans had called for the taking of Caen on June 6. The city did not fall until the end of July.

Canadians were involved in many of the battles in and around Caen, where they fought SS-Oberführer Kurt Meyer's 12th SS panzer Division. Meyer's unit was made up of boys from the Hitler Youth (a Nazi organization for young boys), and they were fanatical, refusing to surrender and forcing the Canadians to fight for every pile of rubble.

In the heat of battle, little mercy was shown by either side, but 156 Canadian prisoners were shot out of hand around Caen in the weeks after D-Day. In 1945, Meyer was found responsible and sentenced to death for war crimes, although he spent only nine years in prison.

Canadian soldiers in Caen

In August, after Caen had fallen, the Canadians and British pushed south to meet the Americans, who had swung round in a huge arc from their invasion beaches. On August 19, the Canadian 4th Armoured Division met up with American forces at Chambois, trapping sixty thousand German troops, almost eight hundred tanks and thousands of vehicles in what became known as the Falaise Pocket.

It was an important victory, but it came at a cost—1,470 Canadians were dead and over four hundred wounded.

Young German prisoners of war

The Day the Soldiers Came

The ruins of Oradour-sur-Glane are preserved as a reminder of the murder of the townsfolk in 1944.

Eight-year-old Roger Godfrin's mother always told him, "When you see the Germans, run away." When the SS came to Roger's school on the afternoon of June 10, 1944, that's exactly what he did.

Robert Hebras and four companions crawled out from beneath a burning pile of bodies and hid in a barn.

Marguerite Rouffanche climbed through a window of the village church and dropped ten feet to the ground.

These were seven of the very few survivors of the day soldiers of the 2nd Waffen-SS Panzer Division Das Reich came to Oradour-sur-Glane.

As a reprisal for local resistance activity after D-Day, the SS collected the inhabitants of the village at the local fairground. They split the men into groups and took them to six locations in the village. They crammed the women and children into the church. Then they killed everyone and set the village on fire.

Today, Oradour-sur-Glane is preserved as it was left when the SS departed as a memorial to the 642 innocent people who died that Saturday afternoon.

July 20 Plot

Stauffenberg

Many senior officers in the German army saw Hitler and his Nazis as thugs with little or no class or culture. They grumbled but did little as long as Hitler kept giving them victories. However, as things began to go wrong, several began to think that something had to be done.

As early as March, 1943, an attempt was made on Hitler's life, but the bomb on his plane failed to explode. As the military situation worsened and the Allies landed in France, it became imperative to try something else. An officer who had been seriously wounded in North Africa, Colonel Claus von Stauffenberg, agreed to take a bomb into a meeting with Hitler at his headquarters at Rastenburg on July 20.

Stauffenberg triggered the bomb, left it by Hitler's feet and excused himself from the conference. When the bomb exploded, Stauffenberg assumed Hitler was dead and flew back to Berlin to begin the coup to take over the government.

Damage caused by
the bomb.

But Hitler wasn't dead. Another officer, annoyed when he'd kicked Stauffenberg's briefcase, had moved it to the other side of a heavy table leg. Although four others at the table died, the leg saved Hitler from the blast, and he lived to phone Berlin. Stauffenberg and three other conspirators were arrested and shot immediately.

In the weeks after July 20, thousands were arrested and tried and hundreds executed, some by being hanged with piano wire. Hitler had some of the executions filmed so he could watch.

The highest profile conspirator was General Rommel, who, because of his fame, was offered the chance to commit suicide rather than be tried and executed. In choosing suicide, Rommel spared his family from execution.

If the briefcase hadn't been moved, Hitler would have been killed, but it would have made little difference. It was too late for a negotiated peace. After all the horror and suffering, only Germany's unconditional surrender would do.

Warsaw Destroyed

Why did the Russians, who for much of the uprising were only across the Vistula Rirver from the fighting, not help the Poles?

Partly, the Russian army was exhausted after its hard-fought advance to the outskirts of Warsaw. But also, Stalin was happy to let his troops sit back and watch the Germans destroy the Polish Home Army. In 1940, Stalin had ordered the murder of tens of thousands of Polish officers in the forests of Katyn. He wanted to take over a passive Poland, where he could install his own government. If the Germans killed off anyone who was prepared to resist him, so much the better.

Although Churchill generally supported the Polish Home Army and allowed Polish and South African pilots in the Royal Air Force to fly long and dangerous missions to drop supplies to the Warsaw fighters, he did not receive support from Roosevelt, who did not want to upset Stalin.

By August, 1944, the Russian army was only fifteen or so kilometres from Warsaw. The ghetto where the Jews had fought heroically a year before was a pile of rubble, but the Polish underground in the rest of the city was ready to rise in revolt against the German occupiers to meet the Russian liberators.

On August 1, the Polish Home Army, armed with only light weapons, rose in rebellion. In hard fighting, they took control of much of the old centre of the city, but failed to take either the airports or the east bank of the Vistula River close to the Russians.

The Home Army had planned for only few days of fighting before linking up with the Russians. Strong German resistance to the uprising and a lack of Russian help left them isolated. The uprising lasted for sixty-three days before the Poles were forced to surrender. In those days, some 16,000 Polish fighters died and over 100,000 civilians were killed.

In revenge, Hitler ordered the city destroyed and the surviving population removed. When the Russians finally entered the city in January, 1945, they found deserted ruins with 85% of the buildings destroyed.

Downtown Warsaw was razed by the defeated Nazis.

Two Attempts, Two Failures

British troops on a bridge at Nijmegen in the the Netherlands

The Germans surrounded the Belgian town of Bastogne and besieged the American troops there. Desperate to take the town so that the Panzers could move on quickly, the German commander asked the outnumbered Americans to surrender.

Brigadier General McAuliffe famously replied with a one word telegram, "Nuts."

The Americans held out until they were relieved by General Patton's tanks.

After Falaise, the Allies swept across France, liberating Paris and pushing through Belgium and into the Netherlands. But supply lines were stretched and the fighting was hard. Something dramatic was needed if there was a chance that the war in Europe could be ended that year.

In September, Operation Market Garden dropped parachute troops to capture bridges over the main rivers in Holland and to outflank the German defences. The plan called for armoured units to race along the road and relieve the parachutists, but resistance was tougher than expected.

Of the three bridges captured, the tanks couldn't reach the third at Arnhem, and the parachutists had to withdraw or be captured. As one of the planners had commented before the operation, they had tried to go a bridge too far.

As Christmas approached, in heavy snow and overcast weather, the Germans tried a desperate gamble to break through the Allied lines in the Ardennes and race to the Channel ports.

At first the Panzers made progress, but when the weather cleared and the Allied planes could fly once more, the German tanks became sitting ducks, and their attack ground to a halt. Both gambles at the end of 1944 failed. The war would go on into 1945.

Iwo Jima

Five days into the battle at Iwo Jima, a group of Marines climbed Mount Suribachi, the highest point on the island, and set up a small American flag.

Shortly after, the flag was replaced by a larger one and the raising photographed. It became one of the most famous pictures ever taken, and the men who were in it heroes. Three of them were later killed in the battle, but the survivors went back to the U.S., where they toured to encourage the buying of war bonds.

Some of the men had trouble adjusting to the fame, most notably Ira Hayes, who turned to alcohol and died aged only thirty-two in 1955. Hayes probably suffered from unrecognized Post Traumatic Stress Disorder.

By February, 1945, the American island-hopping across the Pacific had brought them to Iwo Jima, the first of the Japanese home islands and only 1,200 kilometres from Tokyo.

With no navy left, the over twenty thousand Japanese defenders could only let the American Marines come ashore. But then the situation changed. Hidden bunkers and eighteen kilometres of tunnels were safe from the American artillery fire and had to be cleared individually using grenades and flamethrowers.

The fighting was intense and brutal. Between the landings in February 19 and the time the 21-square-kilometre island was declared secure thirty-five days later, 21,703 Japanese and 6,821 Americans soldiers were dead.

Many of the Japanese defenders committed suicide rather than surrender, and some lived on in the tunnel complex long after the fighting ended. The last two surrendered in 1951, six years after the battle.

Into Germany

In 1943, Princess Juliana, the daughter of the Dutch queen, moved to Ottawa to escape the bombing of London, where her family was in exile.

Princess Juliana was pregnant, and when she gave birth to a daughter, Margriet, the Canadian government declared the floor she was on in Ottawa's Civic Hospital to be Dutch territory so that the baby, who was in line for the Dutch throne, could technically be born in the Netherlands.

The christening of Princess Margriet in Ottawa

After the failure of Market Garden in the Netherlands, the two corps of the First Canadian Army, working together for the first time, were given the task of clearing the Scheldt estuary and opening the port of Antwerp. Despite five weeks of bitter fighting in October and November, 1944 and heavy casualties as they struggled through flooded countryside and over heavily defended canals, the Canadians succeeded. Then an unusually severe winter set in.

That winter in the Netherlands was known as the "Hunger Winter", and some ten thousand Dutch men, women and children died. As spring arrived, a truce was arranged with the Germans to allow the Royal Air Force and the American Air Force to drop food to the starving population. Thundering in as low as 120 metres above ground, huge Lancaster and Flying Fortress bombers dropped eleven thousand tons of food and saved countless lives.

As the spring weather arrived, the Allies forced their way over the Rhine River, opening the way into Germany itself.

For their part, the Canadian First Army continued into the Netherlands to liberate that county. They established a special relationship with the Dutch that lasts to this day.

A Lancaster bomber

71

Missiles and Rockets

The Gloster Meteor

By 1944, the Luftwaffe had long since lost the capacity to bomb London as it had during the Blitz in 1940 and 1941. But new and terrifying weapons were on their way.

The V-1 was an early version of the cruise missile. It used a very noisy pulse-jet engine and was launched either from a ramp on the ground or a bomber in flight. They were small and very fast, making them difficult to shoot down. Londoners soon realized that you could hear the V-1s coming but that as soon as the engine cut out, the silence meant that the bomb was on its way down.

The British rushed the Gloster Meteor, the Allies' first jet fighter, into service to combat the V-1 threat, and their battles over the south of England were the first combat where jet aircraft were used.

About ten thousand V-1s were fired at England, with 2,419 reaching London and killing over six thousand people. Frightening though the V-1 was, there was worse.

The launch of a V-2 rocket

The V-2 was the world's first ballistic missile. Dropping on its target from one hundred kilometres up at greater than the speed of sound, it gave no warning and was impossible to stop. Over three thousand V-2s were fired at targets in Europe, killing 7,250 people.

Terrifying though these new weapons were, they were inaccurate and had no effect on the course of the war. However, the technology was absorbed by the victorious Russians and Americans, and much of it found its way into the missiles that threatened the world during the Cold War.

To Berlin

As the Germans were being surrounded at Falaise, they were also suffering their greatest losses of the war in the east. The Russian Operation Bagratian in Belorussia cost them hundreds of thousands of soldiers, thousands of tanks and pushed them back to their 1941 borders.

The German army never recovered from Falaise, and Bagratian and could only slow the Allied advances. In January, 1945, the Russian Army began its final push on Berlin, the capital of Germany.

The battle for the ruins of Berlin itself began on April 20, Hitler's fifty-sixth birthday. It was brutal, costing the lives of almost half a million German soldiers and an unknown number of civilians. During the battle and in

The damaged Reichstag, once a symbol of German pride

the aftermath, perhaps as many as 100,000 women were raped by Russian soldiers.

While old men and boys fought for what was left of his capital, Hitler lived in a bunker deep beneath the ruins of the Chancellery. Completely out of touch with reality, he ordered armies that no longer existed to fight on and raged against the betrayals he thought had brought him there. On April 29, he married his mistress, Eva Braun. The following day, with the Russians less than half a kilometre away, Hitler and his new wife committed suicide.

On May 2, the Russians raised their flag in the ruins of the Reichstag, the old parliament building in central Berlin, and the battle ended.

On April 25, Russian and American soldiers had met on the Elbe River, cutting what was left of Germany in half. On May 8, the fighting ended, and the war in Europe was over.

Not Yet the End

The *Yamato*

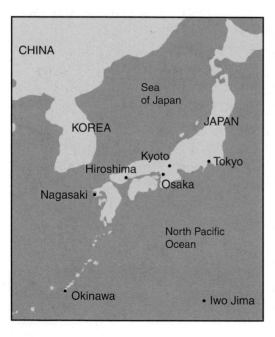

While Europe celebrated, the war in the Pacific continued. In March, the U.S. forces invaded Okinawa, only five hundred kilometres from the main Japanese islands. The Japanese responded with the largest Kamikaze suicide attacks of the war, sinking dozens of ships. The biggest battleship in the world was also sent on a suicide mission.

The *Yamato* was longer than two football fields, had armour almost half a metre thick, and guns that could hurl a high-explosive, armour-piercing shell forty-two kilometres. The plan was for the *Yamato* to run aground on the shores of Okinawa, a large island, and use its huge guns to wreak havoc among the invading Americans. On April 7, it was attacked by almost four hundred aircraft. Its magazines exploded and it sank.

Meanwhile, on Okinawa, the Japanese fought fanatically for eighty-two days. When Okinawa fell at the end of June, over twelve thousand Americans and two hundred thousand Japanese, half of them civilians, were dead.

Okinawa gave a sense of what it would be like to invade the big Japanese islands. Hundreds of thousands would die in months of horrific fighting. However, early in the morning of July 16, something happened in the remote New Mexico desert that would not only make the invasion of Japan unnecessary but would change forever the nature of war.

Hiroshima and Nagasaki

What happened in New Mexico was Trinity, the first test explosion of a nuclear weapon.

The Trinity bomb exploded with the force of 20,000 tons of conventional explosive and created a mushroom cloud 12 kilometers in height, a shockwave that was felt 160 kilometres away and a flash that lit up the sky 240 kilometres away. The sand below the bomb was fused into a light green radioactive glass.

As he watched the test, J. Robert Oppenheimer, the director of the Manhattan Project responsible for creating the bomb, was reminded of a line from Hindu scripture, "I am become Death, the destroyer of worlds."

Oppenheimer

The American bomb took fifty-seven seconds to fall from the plane to its detonation height of six hundred metres. In the 58th second, everything and everybody within 1.6 kilometers of the point below the bomb was utterly destroyed. It was 8:15 on the morning of August 6, 1945, and the Japanese city of Hiroshima had gained the tragic distinction of being the first city in the world to be attacked by nuclear weapons.

The Hiroshima bomb, Little Boy, was not the same as the one tested in Trinity. It was simpler and less powerful. Nevertheless, seventy thousand people died that day, and about the same number died of the radiation effects before the year was out.

Hiroshima had not been heavily bombed, so most of the wooden buildings had not burned in firestorms. They provided no protection from the searing heat and violent shockwave. People close to the explosion simply ceased to exist, sometimes leaving only shadows on walls or steps.

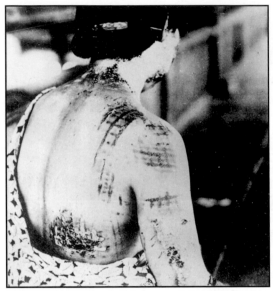

This woman's clothing pattern was burned into her skin.

Those farther away were burned, sometimes having the patterns on their clothes burned onto their skin. What confused the Japanese doctors most was why people died for no apparent reason long after the bombing. They had never seen radiation sickness before.

On August 8th, Russia declared war on Japan and invaded the Japanese territories in Manchuria. On the same day, a second bomb, Fat Man, exploded over another city, Nagasaki. Faced with this terrifying new weapon, on August 15, a surrender message from Emperor Hirohito was broadcast on Japanese radio. Some extremists in the army tried to prevent the message being read but, for the first time in history, a Japanese Emperor spoke directly to his people. On September 2, the Japanese government signed the surrender documents aboard the American battleship USS *Missouri*. WWII was officially over.

The Nagasaki "mushrom cloud"

The Japanese sign their surrender

The Cost

The Memorial to the Murdered Jews of Europe by architect Peter Eisenman was opened in Berlin in 2004. It consists of a 19,000 square metre site covered with 2,711 concrete slabs arranged in a grid pattern on a slope.

Over seventy million people died in WW II. They came from fifty-five countries, and more than half of them were civilians.

Sixteen per cent of the 1939 population of Poland, over five million people, including three million Jews, died, as did twenty-three million Russians, twenty million Chinese, over seven million Germans and almost three million Japanese. A million Yugoslavs died, as did a million Vietnamese. Britain and the United States suffered over four hundred thousand deaths each. Eight hundred thousand Romanians perished and, at the other end of the scale, three hundred Mongolians and a hundred Swiss never saw 1945. Closer to home, 45,300 Canadian soldiers and one thousand from Newfoundland alone never came home.

The figures are numbing, but every single one of those seventy-three million was a person, a mother, child, brother, sister, father. Some died willingly for what they believed in, some were doing a hard job that had to be done, and countless millions simply wanted to live in peace and were caught up in forces they couldn't control and could barely understand. Millions died simply because they were Jewish, and more millions starved because the war didn't allow them to grow enough food to live.

Guilt

Despite all the rules of war that people devise, crimes happen on all sides. The murder of prisoners and the rape of women were relatively common in the Pacific war. Even in Europe there were a number of cases, one in Sicily involving Canadian soldiers, where soldiers shot prisoners out of hand. Some would argue that the firestorm bombing of the lightly defended city of Dresden in 1945 was a war crime. But scale becomes a factor, and nothing can compare to the horror of the death camps and the deliberate murder of six million people in them.

After the war, the Allies convened a trial at Nuremberg to assess the guilt of the Nazi leaders. Twenty-four were tried and twelve sentenced to death by hanging. Other trials of hundreds of Nazis were carried out in the years after the war. The most famous was the trial of Adolf Eichmann, the man who had been Heydrich's assistant at Wannsee and who was responsible for the efficient transportation of millions of Jews to the death camps. Eichmann was found guilty and hanged on May 31, 1962.

After the defeat of Japan, trials were held all across Asia. Nine hundred and twenty war criminals were executed for crimes which included the execution and torture of prisoners, illegal medical experiments and cannibalism.

Nazi leaders on trial at Nuremberg, including Hermann Göring, the former head of the Luftwaffe, Hess and von Ribbentrop, the former foreign minister

Aftermath

At the end of WW II, both the Americans and Russians rushed to get their hands on German technology and the German scientists who had worked on jet fighters and rockets. They did this because they knew another war was coming.

Russia created an empire of puppet states out of the countries it liberated in 1944 and 1945. The United States made alliances where necessary to try and stop the expansion of both Russia and China. By the 1950s, both Russia and America had enough nuclear weapons to destroy the world. The fear each had for the other made it a Cold War with no direct fighting between the major powers, but that did not mean there was no fighting.

In 1950, the Korean War broke out and caused the deaths of about two million people, including 516 Canadians. The Vietnam War lasted from 1959 to 1975, causing over a million more casualties. The war in Afghanistan lasted from 1978 to 1988, with consequences that are killing Canadians and Afghans there today.

The Cold War ended with the collapse of Soviet Russia in 1989, but many of today's conflicts still owe their origins to the Second World War. Just as we can't understand WW II without knowing about WW I, we can't understand what's happening in our world today without understanding WW II.

The Hiroshima Peace Memorial Park

Timeline of WW II

1919, January 15	Rosa Luxemburg is murdered.
1921, July 29	Adolf Hitler becomes leader of the Nazi Party.
1922	Benito Mussolini seizes power in Italy.
1933, January 30	Adolf Hitler is elected Chancellor of Germany.
1936, July 18	General Franco leads a military revolt in Spain.
1936	The Olympics take place in Berlin.
1937	Japan, already in Manchuria, invades central China.
1937, April 26	Guernica is bombed.
1938	Hitler annexes Austria and western Czechoslovakia.
1939 August	Germany and Russia sign a non-aggression pact.
1939, September 1	Germany invades Poland, WW II begins.
1939, September 3	Britain and France declare war on Germany.
1939, September 10	Canada declares war on Germany.
1939, September 17	Russia invades eastern Poland.
1939, October 6	Polish forces surrender.
1939, November 30	Russia invades Finland.
1939, December 17	*Graf Spee* is scuttled.
1940, April 8	Germany invades Denmark and Norway.
1940, May 10	Germany invades France, Holland, Belgium and Luxembourg. Winston Churchill becomes Britain's prime minister.
1940, May 20	German Panzers reach the English Channel, cutting off the Allied armies in Belgium.
1940, May 27	Evacuation of British and French forces from Dunkirk begins.
1940, June 4	Dunkirk evacuation ends, 338,000 troops are rescued.
1940, June 10	Italy declares war on France and Britain.
1940, June 14	German troops enter Paris.
1940, June 18	Russia invades Lithuania, Latvia and Estonia.
1940, June 22	France surrenders.
1940, July 10	The Battle of Britain begins.
1940, August 25	British bombers attack Berlin.
1940, September	The Luftwaffe's objective changes from defeating the RAF to bombing London, and the Blitz begins.
1940, September 13	Italy invades Egypt.
1940, September 17	Hitler postpones the invasion of Britain.
1940, September 18	*City of Benares* torpedoed.
1940, September 27	Japan joins Germany and Italy in the Axis.
1940, October 28	Italy invades Greece.
1940, December 9	British forces counterattack the Italians in North Africa.

1941, February 12	Hitler sends Rommel and the Afrika Korps to help the Italians in North Africa.
1941, April 6	Germany invades Yugoslavia and Greece.
1941, April 27	German troops occupy Athens.
1941, May 9	U-boat *U-110* is captured with Enigma machine and code books.
1941, May 10	Rudolf Hess parachutes into a Scottish field.
1941, June 22	Germany invades Russia.
1941, September 15	The German siege of Leningrad begins.
1941, October 2	The final German attack towards Moscow begins.
1941, October 15	Rains and mud stop the German advance on Moscow.
1941, November 30	The Germans get within 27 km of Moscow.
1941, December 6	The Russians counterattack outside Moscow in temperatures of -30C°.
1941, December 7	The Japanese navy attacks Pearl Harbor.
1941, December 10	*Prince of Wales* and *Repulse* sunk by Japanese bombers.
1941, December 11	Germany and Italy declare war on the US. It is now truly a world war.
1941, December 25	Hong Kong surrenders.
1942, January 12	Japanese forces invade Burma.
1942, January 20	The Wannsee Conference.
1942, January 21	Rommel begins another offensive in North Africa.
1942, February 15	Singapore surrenders to the Japanese.
1942. March 20	Large-scale murder of Jews in camps begins.
1942, April 18	Doolittle's raid on Tokyo.
1942, May 7	Battle of the Coral Sea
1942, May 6	American troops in the Philippines surrender.
1942, May 8	German offensive in southern Russia begins
1942, May 27	Heydrich assassinated in Prague.
1942, June 4	The battle of Midway
1942, June 27	Convoy PQ 17 sails.
1942, July 18	ME262, the worlds first jet plane, flies in Germany.
1942, August 13	Montgomery becomes commander of the British 8th army in North Africa.
1942, August 19	The Allied landing at Dieppe fails.
1942, August 23	Germans bomb Stalingrad to open the battle.
1942, October 3	V-2 rocket becomes the first man-made object to reach space.
1942, October 14	The SS *Caribou* is sunk in Cabot Strait.
1942, October 23	The battle of El Alamein begins.
1942, November 8	Allied forces land in western North Africa.
1942, November 19	The Russian counterattack at Stalingrad begins.
1942, November 22	The German 6th Army is surrounded at Stalingrad.

1942, December 19	The Germans attempt to break the encirclement at Stalingrad fails.
1943, January 18	Jews of the Warsaw Ghetto rise in revolt.
1943, February 2	The German 6th Army in Stalingrad surrenders.
1943, May 13	The last Axis forces in North Africa surrender.
1943, May	Resistance in the Warsaw Ghetto is finally overcome.
1943, July 5	The Battle of Kursk begins.
1943, July 10	The Allies invade Sicily.
1943, July 25	Mussolini is replaced and arrested.
1943, September 3	The Allies invade the Italian mainland.
1943, September 8	Italy surrenders. German forces occupy central and northern Italy.
1943, November 6	The Russians liberate Kiev.
1943, Nov./Dec.	The Tehran Conference
1944, January 16	Eisenhower becomes supreme commander of western Allied forces.
1944, January 22	The Allies land at Anzio, Italy.
1944, June 6	D-Day. American, British and Canadian troops land on the beaches of Normandy.
1944, June 10	The massacre at Oradour-sur-Glane
1944, June 12	The First German V-1 missile lands on Britain.
1944. June 19	Battle of the Philippine Sea
1944, July 20	Hitler survives an assassination attempt by senior German officers.
1944, August 1	Warsaw revolts against the Germans.
1944, August 15	The Allies land in southern France.
1944, August 25	Paris is liberated.
1944, September 8	The first German V-2 rocket lands on Britain.
1944, September 17	Operation Market Garden in the Netherlands begins.
1944, October 5	British forces land in Greece.
1944, October 14	Athens is liberated.
1944, October	The Japanese begin to use Kamikaze suicide pilots.
1944, November 14	B-29 bombers begin large-scale bombing of Tokyo.
1944, November 24	The mutiny of Canadian soldiers at Terrace.
1944, December 16	The German attack in the Ardennes begins.
1945, January 9	U.S. Marines land in the Philippines.
1945, January 23	Russians cross the Oder River and enter Germany.
1945, January 27	The Russians liberate Auschwitz.
1945, January 28	The Battle of the Ardennes ends.
1945, February 13	The Russians occupy Budapest. Dresden is bombed.
1945, February 19	U.S. marines land in Iwo Jima.
1945, February	The Yalta Conference

1945, March 7	Western Allies cross the Rhine River into Germany.
1945, March 16	The Battle of Iwo Jima ends.
1945, April 6	U.S. marines land in Okinawa.
1945, April 11	The Allies liberate Buchenwald concentration camp.
1945, April 12	President Roosevelt dies.
1945, April 13	The Russians enter Vienna.
1945, April 25	American and Russian forces meet in Germany.
1945, April 26	German defense in northern Italy collapses.
1945, April 29	Mussolini is executed by the Italian resistance. The Allies liberate Dachau concentration camp.
1945, April 30	Adolf Hitler commits suicide in his bunker in Berlin.
1945, May 8	Germany surrenders. The war in Europe ends.
1945, June 21	The Battle of Okinawa ends.
1945, July 16	The U.S. successfully explodes an atomic bomb in New Mexico.
1945, July/August	The Potsdam Conference
1945, August 6	Hiroshima is destroyed by an atomic bomb.
1945, August 8	Russia declares war on Japan.
1945, August 9	Nagasaki is destroyed by an atomic bomb.
1945, August 14	Japan surrenders. World War II ends.
1945/46	The Nuremberg war crimes trials
1962, May 31	Adolf Eichmann is executed for war crimes.

Resources for learning more about WW II

The following is a selection of the books used by the author in writing this story:

The Battle for Spain by Antony Beevor (New York: Penguin, 2006)

Canada: Our Century by Mark Kingwell and Christopher Moore (Toronto: Doubleday, 1999)

Convoy by Martin Middlebrook (New York: Penguin, 1978)

Days of Victory by Ted Barris and Alex Barris (Toronto: Macmillan, 1995)

Dieppe: 1942 by Ronald Atkin (London: Macmillan, 1980)

Dresden by Frederick Taylor (New York: HarperCollins, 2005)

The Fall of Berlin by Antony Beevor (New York: Penguin, 2002)

The Front Page Story of World War II by Robert R. Reid (Vancouver: Douglas & McIntyre, 1994)

The Gallant Cause by Mark Zuehlke (Vancouver: Whitecap, 1996)

Hitler's War on Russia by Paul Carell (London: Corgi, 1964)

The Holocaust by Martin Gilbert (New York: Henry Holt, 1985)

Military Errors of World War Two by Kenneth Macksey (Toronto: Stoddart, 1987)

Oradour-Sur-Glane: The Tragedy Hour by Hour by Robert Hebras (Montreuil-Bellay: Editions C.M.D., 1994)

Overlord by Max Hastings (New York: Simon and Schuster, 1994)

The Rising Sun by John Toland (New York: Bantam, 1971)

The Road to Stalingrad by John Erickson (London: Weidenfield and Nicolson, 1975)

The Second World War by John Keegan (New York: Penguin, 1989)

Six Armies in Normandy by John Keegan (New York: Penguin, 1983)

Stalingrad by Antony Beevor (New York: Penguin, 1998)

Tank vs Tank by Kenneth Macksey (Topsfiels, MA: Salem House, 1988)

The Unknown War by Harrison E. Salisbury (New York: Bantam, 1978)

Victory at Falaise by Denis Whitaker and Shelagh Whitaker (Toronto: HarperCollins, 2000)

World War II by Simon Adams (New York: Dorling Kindersley, 2000)

WW II on the Web

There is a great deal of information about World War II on the internet. The internet changes every day. At the time that this book was printed, all of these sites were online. However, we can't guarantee that they will always be there. A simple keyword search will take you to information about the war and the history of that era.

http://www.spartacus.schoolnet.co.uk/2WW.htm
A large and very informative site

http://www.warmuseum.ca
Information about the Canadian War Museum in Gatineau, Quebec. A great place to visit for more information and to see exhibits about the war.

http://www.vac-acc.gc.ca/remembers/sub.cfm?source=history/SecondWar
Information about Canada's role in WW II

http://www.secondworldwar.co.uk/
A good and interesting general site about the war.

http://www.ushmm.org/
The United States Holocaust Memorial Museum. An excellent resource of thoughtful material.

http://www.pcf.city.hiroshima.jp/index_e2.html
The Hiroshima Peace Memorial

http://www.annefrank.org/content.asp?pid=1&lid=2
Anne Frank House

http://www.junobeach.org/main.html
Honouring Canadian contributions to WW II

Index

About the Author

Photo by Dayle Sutherland

Born in Edinburgh, Scotland, John Wilson has always been addicted to history and firmly believes that the past must have been just as exciting, confusing and complex to those who lived through it as our world is to us. Every one of his nineteen novels and seven non-fiction books for kids, teens and adults deals with the past.

His tales involve intelligent dinosaurs, Roman Legionnaries, crusader knights, lost explorers and frightened soldiers. His novel about Henry Hudson's voyages, *The Alchemist's Dream*, was shortlisted for the Governor General's Award. John's most recent titles are *Crusade* and *Death on the River*.

John has also written the Weet trilogy for Napoleon, as well as the Stories of Canada titles *Righting Wrongs: The Story of Norman Bethune* and *Discovering the Arctic: The Story of John Rae*, both of which were Norma Fleck Award nominees. *Bitter Ashes* is a companion to *Desperate Glory: The Story of WW I*. John lives on Vancouver Island and you can learn more about his books and his school and library presentations on his blog at: johnwilson-author.blogspot.com.

Stories of Canada
by John Wilson

Righting Wrongs: The Story of Norman Bethune
Discovering the Arctic: The Story of John Rae
Desperate Glory: The Story of WW I

The Stories of Canada Series

More information online at
www.napoleonandcompany.com

Photo Credits